Bobby Walason

Boss Angel
III

Boss Angel
III
By Bobby Walason

Bobby Walason

COPYRIGHT

ALL RIGHTS RESERVED. No portion of this publication may be reproduced or transmitted in any form or fashion or by any means, including but not limited to electronic or mechanical. This prohibition includes photocopying, recording, or any information storage and/or retrieval system whatsoever without permission in writing from the copyright owner, expect for brief quotations for review, for authorized promotional opportunities, or where permitted by law.

The author and the publisher have made every effort to ensure the accuracy and completeness of the information contained herein, though acknowledging some may be partially or totally inaccurate. They assume no responsibilities for errors, inaccuracies, omissions, or inconsistencies. Any slights of people, places, or organizations are purely and solely unintentional. Please do not participate in or encourage piracy.

ISBN: 979-8-8691-6340-0

First Edition: February 2024

Printed in the United States of America by Ingramspark

Published by Robert Walason Publishing

ROBERT WALASON PUBLISHING

Boss Angel III

TABLE OF CONTENTS

Chapter One..06
James Gandolfini

Chapter Two..25
Sam Cooke

Chapter Three...39
Albert Anastasia

Chapter Four...59
Malcolm X

Chapter Five..73
Legs Diamond

Chapter Six..89
Humphrey Bogart

Chapter Seven..107
Jimi Hendrix

Chapter Eight...145
Teddy Pendergrass

Chapter Nine..164
Nicole Brown Simpson

Chapter Ten..188
Michael Jackson

Chapter Eleven..................................267
Martin Luther King Jr.

Chapter Twelve..................................276
Marlon Brando

Chapter Thirteen................................293
Whitney Houston

Chapter One

James Gandolfini

As the Boss Angel awaits the arrival of who will be delivering the next mission, he wonders, "Will it be Maggie or JB?"

Then, all dressed to kill, Maggie has arrived in her double-breasted bolero waist short suit jacket, with a thigh-high skirt, and black leather boots just below the knee. She completes her look with tight black fishnet stockings, looking as fine as possible.

For the first time, Boss Angel sees Maggie with her hair up and dyed black. She adorns quadruple braids tucked behind her head. Her outfit is black leather, matching her boots. Boss Angel remarks, "I cannot believe the tough guy look you're sporting." He instantly begins to wonder, as she approaches the bar, what type of mission they are about to undertake.

Maggie approaches Boss Angel with a big, huge hug, and he begins to wonder, "Could it possibly be the beginning of an Angel love, half-Angel type relationship?"

Or is it just the fact that he hasn't seen her in the last five missions due to Achilles and JB hogging the saves? "OK, come on Maggie, the suspense is killing me. What is the next mission?"

"OK, let me ask you a question. Do you remember a quote from Tony Soprano, otherwise known as James Gandolfini? James Gandolfini once said that playing a stockbroker or lawyer did not interest him. He wanted to play everyday people like his parents. His father was a bricklayer-cement mason who eventually became the head custodian of a high school. His mother was the head lunch lady of a high school. James respected his hardworking parents who enabled him to go to college and get a good education."

These were the kind of people James Gandolfini loved and wanted to portray in movies.

"Oh my God, Maggie, please tell me we will be diving into The Sopranos family with James Gandolfini as our mission target? Please, Maggie, tell me it's true."

"Wow, I guess you're a huge fan, which means you'll give it everything you've got and try everything in your power to save Gandolfini!"

"So, Maggie, when will we meet, and will it be at the Bada Bing! If that's the case, you'll be there on your own!"

OK, let's get back to it. During his audition for The Sopranos, it was known that he sat down and read. Then he bolted in the middle of the audition, stating he was not doing it right. He expressed his desire to leave, come back, and try it again. The producers allowed him to leave and come back to do the audition again. He read the whole thing through, and it was clear to everyone that he was the only real choice for Tony Soprano.

Tony Soprano was a selfish guy who damaged a lot of people's lives as the Boss and obviously wasn't a faithful husband. However, Jim Gandolfini was actually the opposite. People close to him say it was sometimes hard for him to portray such a brutal man and inhabit that mindset. Though as each episode passed, he became a natural and fell right into the Soprano lifestyle.

Bobby Walason

While filming True Romance, written by Quentin Tarantino, James was required to film a particularly violent scene, one of Tarantino's most violent. James said of that scene, "Even if it's the 18th hour of the day and you've been working all week, it's got to be right."

"The scene between James' character, Virgil, and Patricia Arquette's character, Alabama, required him to choke her. She spits in his face, and the scene is fantastic. It takes your breath away."

"Maggie, I have to admit that James Gandolfini shocked me with each and every new role he took on. I could not believe how he could turn his character into something you could not believe he could do."

"I know exactly what you mean, Boss Angel. It appeared that he searched for opposites to test himself, and each time he was the winner!"

James Gandolfini had a very warped sense of humor that a lot of people enjoyed. He once left his co-star Lorraine Bracco, what she called a "stuffed cock," a rooster in her makeup trailer.

"Tony Soprano had all the best qualities of James Gandolfini, and that's why we loved him so much. James was a very soft, kind, almost hippie kind of guy. Brutality and cruelty got to him."

John Travolta said that James was there for him when he lost his son. James flew to Florida and would not leave until Travolta was okay. He stayed for a week with John Travolta in Florida.

John said, "The idea that someone in their profession would go out of their way was one of the many great things about Jimmy."

Although "The Sopranos" was a very successful TV show by that time, Gandolfini really wanted to work with Robert Redford on "The Last Castle." Gandolfini said of his time working with Redford, "He's a very normal, down-to-earth man and very smart. He puts you at ease right away, and that was wonderful. I was very honored actually to work with Robert Redford, and I would have done anything."

"Maggie, I know you must have seen 'The Last Castle,' the prison movie with Gandolfini and Robert Redford. It was one of the most exciting movies I've seen Gandolfini in. Just another example, Maggie, that when it came to acting, James Gandolfini was a true chameleon."

"He is what he is, which is a great actor," to quote Roger Ebert. Redford and Gandolfini are two reasons the movie plays so well. Redford because of what he does, or should I say, what is expected of him - a very strong and unbreakable leader.

Gandolfini, on the other hand, does what is not expected and creates not simply a villain, but a portrait of a type that is so nuanced, so compelling, so instinctively right, that we are looking at the performance of a career.

Hey Boss, I know you remember, and we can't possibly forget his scene-stealing performance in "The Mexican!" Considering that the movie starred Julia Roberts and Brad Pitt. At one point, James wanted to quit his role in "The Mexican" because he thought he wasn't cutting it. Julia Roberts famously was quoted as saying, "He's a liar, he was a genius from the moment he arrived."

Gore Verbinski, the director of "The Mexican," said James's performance is literally so good, and there were times they would forget to say cut because he was so engrossed in watching his performance. He's able to go to a place that's so real at any moment.

"The Sopranos became a television icon, showcasing gritty locations and aging industrial cities such as Elizabeth, Newark, and Paterson, New Jersey. These cities served as the backdrop for many of the filming locations, which have become household names, including the Bada Bing. The Bada Bing even became a popular dance club during and after shooting. It was Tony's office, where they often spoke a little too openly, unlike the real mob who learned to be more discreet over time.

Come on, Maggie, why don't we land right inside the Bada Bing? What do you say? I know you can handle the situation! After all, you're a mighty Arch Angel!"

Alright, let's give it a shot, Boss Angel. But I'll tell you right now, if there's any sleazy nonsense or gangsterism happening, we're out of there in half a second. Agree?

Maggie, it's just a TV show. There's nothing to fear!

Oh no, it's not. I've done my homework, Boss Angel. That is the headquarters of a New York crime family who happened to allow the Sopranos set to shoot the series inside!

Okay, Maggie, I guess you know a lot more than I do. That's why you're the Archangel and I'm only half.

So, are we headed to the Bada Bing?

The exact second Boss Angel says Bada Bing, Maggie snaps her fingers, and suddenly they're at the bar with girls dancing and real wise guys walking around the joint.

There is no filming going on at the moment, so Maggie immediately wants to leave. "I don't feel any reason to stay here. There's nothing going on, and there's nothing to gain. We need to find Gandolfini!" Maggie suggests dropping in on his home in New Jersey, where they do a lot of filming.

Maggie agrees and zaps them to the Soprano home. As they walk up the driveway, they realize that this is where all the cameras are shooting that day. "Maggie, listen. We have to act as extras and pretend we were hired by the production company. This might allow us into the house so we can check on Gandolfini."

Maggie notices a lot of people in the backyard and signals Boss Angel to come around the side of the house to the pool. Once in the back, both Angel and Maggie notice that James Gandolfini appears very nauseous and is throwing up in the pool.

Everyone rushed to his rescue, but he insisted he was okay and that it would pass. Just as he uttered those words, he suddenly collapsed next to the pool, unconscious. Christopher Moltisanti, also known as Michael Imperioli, quickly came to his aid and began performing CPR. It was time for Boss Angel to step in.

"Maggie, give me a few of those tablets that Achilles gave you before we left!" Boss Angel urgently requested. Maggie frantically searched through her pocketbook, struggling to find the tablets. James's condition was deteriorating rapidly, turning blue.

Finally, Maggie pulled out the bag of pills, discreetly turning around to conceal them from view. Meanwhile, Boss Angel joined forces with Chris in administering CPR, desperately trying to revive James.

She walks over to Boss Angel and kneels down beside Gandolfini. Secretly, she palms the pills into Boss Angel's hand. Boss Angel asks, "Can I take over?" Chris questions, "Who are you anyway?" Boss Angel responds, "I'm the doctor for the set. The other one is sick, and I took his place. But forget all that. Let's focus on saving him."

Boss Angel proceeds to give mouth-to-mouth resuscitation while discreetly sliding the pills into Gandolfini's mouth, one at a time, and then all at once. Gandolfini gasps for air and regains consciousness. Within minutes, he stands up as if nothing had ever happened.

It appeared to be a miracle, which in actuality it was. He came back to life in a way that only he could, with the help of Maggie and Boss Angel. With a sense of relief, they slowly walked back to the front of the house, knowing that he was going to be okay and had much to be grateful for.

Suddenly, they hear Gandolfini's voice calling from the side of the house, "Come here, you two!" Maggie and Boss Angel turn around and walk over to James, asking, "What can we do for you?"

James responds, "What do you mean, 'What can you do for me'? Look at what you've already done! I just want to thank both of you, whoever you are, for saving my life. I sincerely appreciate it."

Maggie says to James, "Just a little CPR goes a long way, you know!" James looks at her with a suspicious expression, responding, "I know it took more than that. I don't know how you brought me back, but if you'd like to visit the set anytime, here's my number." Gandolfini hands them a business card.

Maggie replies, "I may take you up on that, and I know Gino would be all for it." James expresses his gratitude, saying, "Well, thanks again. I appreciate it. God bless you."

Maggie and Boss Angel walked down the driveway, passing by the same area where Tony picks up his papers in the morning. Suddenly, in a puff, they disappeared. Gandolfini witnessed the entire event and began to wonder if there is indeed life after death. He shook his head, contemplating the possibilities, and then made his way back towards the house.

Chapter Two

Sam Cooke

Maggie and Boss Angel are in the Biltmore, sipping on a couple of martinis, waiting for Achilles to arrive with the next mission for Boss Angel. Then suddenly, he appears in a chair right there! Achilles apologizes, "There was heavy turbulence I had to conquer." We are very curious why you had to deliver this mission in person?

Sam Cooke was one of the most famous pop stars ever. He was considered equal to Elvis Presley. Sam was sought after by just about every producer in the business because he had that one-of-a-kind voice, and he wrote 90% of his own songs, totaling around 200. A gold mine for just about any producer.

His popularity wasn't only with the public alone, as he became great friends with Muhammad Ali, Jim Brown, and even Malcolm X. They were very close and watched each other's backs throughout their relationship. What all four had in common was the fight for civil rights, and their efforts proved to be worthwhile.

Even Martin Luther King asked Sam for permission to use his song 'A Change Is Gonna Come'. Martin turned that song into his favorite and used it during 'The March on Washington' and many other of his powerful sermons!

Only he and his good friend Ray Charles had an understanding that went beyond just the songs. In fact, each of them understood the importance of production, including the significance of writing and remaining faithful to the artist's vision. Sam was not only a great artist but also a very intelligent man. He put together his own music labels and invited various artists to join him. He recruited so many artists to his label that he surpassed Barry Gordy and his popular Motown sound.

However, despite Sam's apparent success and glorious life, the truth couldn't have been further from that.

When Sam was invited to be on the Dick Clark show in 1963, after his performance of 'Cupid', he sat down with Dick and he asked him, "What would you like to do in the future now that you've conquered the music world?" Sam simply replied, "I would like all of the talent that I am connected with to have hit songs!"

Sam decided to hire an accountant named Allen Klein, who had previously been involved with The Rolling Stones and was actually responsible for the breakup of The Beatles. Two of them stayed with Klein, and two of them went their own way. In other words, he was a devious thief and took money from anyone he worked with.

Even to this day, Paul McCartney and Ringo Starr still carry a special hatred towards Klein because of the damage he caused. Mick Jagger from The Rolling Stones doesn't want to play any of their earliest songs because he knows someone would still be making money off of them through Klein.

Sam was manipulated by Allen Klein to start a new company that would supposedly help save money on taxes and for other untrue reasons. Due to the trust Sam had in him, he went along with everything Klein asked.

On the night of December 11, 1964, Sam went to a couple of nightclubs. The last club he was seen in was PJ's. Eventually, they both ended up at the Hacienda hotel, a real seedy place. The girl claimed Sam was being aggressive, and when he went into the bathroom, she not only grabbed her own clothes but also took Sam's clothes with her and disappeared into the night. When Sam came out of the bathroom, he realized she was gone and that his clothes were also missing. He then found a bathrobe and hurried down to the office, where he asked the hotel manager, Roberta Franklin, if she had seen an Asian girl come down the stairs or anywhere, for that matter. Roberta replied, "No, I haven't seen anybody at all."

Sam went out to the parking lot and checked his car, looking around everywhere, but she was nowhere to be found. His clothes were also missing.

So, Sam returned to the hotel office, and according to Roberta Franklin, the manager, she claimed that he pushed the door in because she was trying to stop him from entering. She further claimed that once he approached her, they started wrestling and she accused him of punching her. However, everyone knew that Sam was a kind-hearted person and would have never punched anyone.

The manager claimed that she was in danger for her life somehow and reached for a gun that was near the counter. She pulled the trigger three times. Unfortunately, one of the three bullets was fatal. It entered Sam's underarm, traveled through his left lung and heart, and exited through the other lung. It was a short period of time before he passed away.

The death of Sam Cooke was declared as a case of self-defense. It was determined that there was no weapon, no gun, no knife, or anything whatsoever found on Sam's body or in the vicinity of his body.

Most of Sam's friends and relatives claimed that Allen Klein had something to do with his death, and many would like to believe that. However, the investigation showed that there were no blood drippings into or out of the hotel office. Still, no one truly knows what happened that night, and it is difficult to understand because Sam had no need for a prostitute, nor would he enter such a terribly seedy hotel like the Hacienda. Even if he did have a date or a prostitute with him that night, he simply wouldn't lower himself to that level!

Boss Angel is summoned by the Archangel Achilles, who orders him back to the Providence Biltmore. Achilles tells him that he has a special extra mission for him, to replace one of the missions Boss Angel failed to complete. Achilles explains that this is not something they usually do, but Sam Cooke was a good soul and didn't deserve his demise. Furthermore, the 'Big Guy' (referring to God) is a huge fan of Sam Cooke. Therefore, Achilles wants Boss Angel to immediately go and save Sam Cooke before anything else. By saving Sam Cooke, Boss Angel will gain three extra souls, whether he needs them or not, although Achilles hopes that he won't.

Boss Angel remembers Sam Cooke as one of his all-time favorite singers, so there are multiple reasons to save him aside from admiration. He also knows that he's currently at -2 on his saves, and by saving Sam, he'll be able to increase that count by one. Sam arrives on December 10th, the day before he was killed—or rather, murdered. He wants to arrive early to pay Alan Klein an unexpected visit, but he doesn't want to go when he's in his office. Boss Angel decides it would be better to enter late at night to search for the forged documents that give Klein complete control over everything Sam owned.

Boss Angel takes the elevator and comes out right outside Alan Klein's office, which was previously Sam Cooke's production office. He picks the lock and goes inside, only to find that there are surprisingly only two file cabinets. To his surprise, the first one he slides out contains all the necessary documents he needs.

The next evening, Boss Angel headed to PJ's nightclub, knowing that Sam had reportedly been there the evening he died. Boss Angel enters the nightclub, and it was packed. There weren't many white people, and he caught many stares from the regulars. As he looked around, he spotted a big crowd in the far corner, and there was Sam dancing in the middle. Boss Angel had figured out a good way to approach Sam, so he walked over to him while waving one of the documents over his head. This immediately caught Sam's attention. Boss Angel beckoned him over, and Sam's curiosity drew him toward Boss Angel.

They introduced themselves, and then Boss Angel told him, "I am a good friend of Mick Jagger, you know, the one who got robbed by Alan Klein, not to mention The Beatles. Well, I have a deal for you." Sam became a little paranoid and asked, "Who the hell are you anyway, and how did you get my documents?" Boss Angel replied, "Let's just say I have a vendetta against Alan Klein, but my sole purpose is to save you from harm, more than the cash."

I know you are one of the best singers of these times, and because of that, I need to protect you just until tomorrow when these documents clear and you regain your name on your corporations, your publishing, and all your copyrights. This will happen, Sam, but you must listen to me. I'm only asking for 24 hours. The deal sounded so good to Sam that he said, "OK, but where do we go?" I'm going to take you to a five-star hotel on the other side of town, and I will stay by your side to protect you until the 24 hours expire. Reluctantly, Sam agrees to go to the hotel. All the dancing made him a little tired, and he was looking forward to a nice rest.

The following morning, they have breakfast together, watch a movie in the lobby, then have lunch and dinner. Boss Angel stands up and assures Sam that everything is all set and there's nothing to worry about with Alan Klein any longer. Change these documents to your name and use your own notary, and never go back to that office again. Sam tells Boss Angel once again, "I don't know who you are or where you're from, but you feel like some sort of angel to me, and I'll never forget what you've done once I find out exactly what you've done. Thanks, Boss Angel." Boss Angel takes a drag of his cigarette and says to Sam, "I may or may not be an angel, but right now I'm just a 'Cupid'."

Chapter Three
Albert Anastasia

When Boss Angel received his mission from Maggie, he was in total shock because he had actually done business with this person in the past. It was a name that was well-known from coast to coast, mainly because Boss Angel had worked with him in his early days, particularly in New York City. The person's name was Albert Anastasia, an original Italian American mobster, hitman, and crime boss. This association eventually led him to become the boss of Murder Incorporated and the founder of the modern American Mafia. He served as the underboss of Carlos Gambino and later rose to the position of mob boss in what would become the modern Gambino family. Albert Anastasia was widely regarded as one of the most ruthless and feared organized crime figures in the history of America.

He was born on September 26, 1902, in Parahelia, Italy. His assassination was planned for October 25th, 1957, at the Park Central Hotel in New York City. He had two children, Jack Halloran and Anthony Anastasia Jr.

His parents were Louisa Norlina Philippi and Raffaele Anastasia. From the same neighborhood came the Gallo brothers, and the most eccentric one was Joe Gallo, who earned the nickname 'Crazy

Joe.' He was infamous for being part of the crew behind the shooting of boss Joe Columbo during the Italian American Association gathering in Columbus Circle. However, he was nowhere near as feared as the ruthless hitman Albert Anastasia. Heading Murder Inc, a violent battalion, left no doubt that the Mafia was responsible for the numerous violent murders in the New York area.

One of the members of Murder Incorporated was none other than Charles "Lucky" Luciano, whose reputation was on par with that of Anastasia. He became the head of the notorious organization, handpicked by Lucky Luciano himself, the Godfather of the modern mafia. Therefore, when Lucky Luciano was sentenced to 30 years in prison,

Thomas Dewey's initial impulse was the same as Anastasia's—to seek retaliation or even murder. However, such actions were against the rules at the time. If Thomas Dewey had been assassinated, it is almost certain that the top-level mobsters in New York City would have faced immense pressure from city, state, and federal authorities. Among them, Albert Anastasia stood out as the most dangerous figure in the underworld. It would have been a disastrous career move for the mobsters involved, considering Dewey's relentless war on organized crime. At the top of that list was Albert Anastasia, who was known for his close ties to Louis Buchalter, a friend he ultimately had murdered.

But when the Commission faced continued pressure from authorities, anyone could be deemed expendable. In November 1936, the Mafia found itself in a dire situation with a murder charge hanging over one of its members, the charter. This individual went on the run. Anastasia, fearing that his friend and partner could face a fate similar to that of Luciano, if not worse, called upon the Murder Incorporated network to ensure Lucky's safe hiding. As word got out, it became known that if you were elected, you would be next on Dewey's hit list.

Now, here he had seen Schultz get killed, witnessed Luciano go to jail, and found himself in hiding. Bernard Whalen, the author of undisclosed police files, had no idea of his whereabouts. Some speculated he was overseas in Jerusalem, but as it turned out, he had been in Brooklyn all along. In an attempt to rattle Prosecutor Thomas Dewey, who had intensified the pressure by offering a $25,000 reward for Legs' capture, Anastasia decided to take matters into his own hands. He aimed to dismantle Dewey's case using the only method he knew - a list of informants provided by Lepke, meant to expose the rats involved.

He put Murder Incorporated to work, eliminating key witnesses. He was the kind of person who believed that witnesses had to be eliminated, and if anyone unfortunate enough to witness him commit a murder, they would be killed as well. This ruthless approach may have contributed to his success. He understood that leaving no witnesses behind was a fundamental principle for him.

In order to establish his legitimacy, he began working on the docks. Keep in mind that he was a formidable man, and the person in charge of the docks was Joe Torino. No work was conducted without going through Joe. Anastasia gave Joe Torino such a severe beating in front of the entire group of dockworkers that it resulted in Torino's death. Immediately after the altercation, Anastasia was arrested and charged with murder. He was eventually sentenced to death. The brutality with which he enjoyed beating that man to death instilled even greater fear in the hearts of those who witnessed it.

While in prison, he became even more feared, as if he had lost his soul. He gained a reputation as the toughest and most dangerous man in all of New York. Even on death row, he didn't attempt to tamper with himself. Most guys in that situation try to make amends, giving the guards and fellow inmates an easier time. Many of them express regret and wish they weren't there. However, he took the opposite approach. He continued to engage in violent behavior, beating up fellow inmates. This caught the attention of the prison's barber, who had earned the nickname "the Shiv." It's unclear how he became a barber in there, but it's certain that "the Shiv" had other roles too. He acted as a scout for criminal gangs outside the prison, and he believed Anastasia's skills would be a perfect fit for a specific client: a rising lieutenant in one of New York's most powerful Italian gangs, Charles "Lucky" Luciano. Lucky Luciano epitomized the qualities needed to become a boss.

He knew what he wanted and had no fear of pursuing it. As the head of Murder Incorporated and their killing squad, he employed members who were not only skilled at their jobs but also took great pride in their work. Now, the time had come to enter the lucrative alcohol market, and Charlie's exceptional business mind made him the perfect candidate. The Volstead Act, which enacted prohibition in the 1920s, prohibited the production, distribution, and sale of alcohol. However, there was a significant loophole - people would continue to consume alcohol as long as they could obtain it. This created a golden opportunity for organized crime, as the demand for alcohol surged. To meet this demand, a reliable supply was crucial. Therefore, Luciano aimed to control the source from which illegal alcohol flowed into the Brooklyn docks.

Luciano decided to enlist his attorneys to have Anastasia's life sentence dismissed, exploiting a technicality, and remarkably, it worked. Now, a transformed Anastasia found himself under the influence of Charlie Luciano, who controlled all the strings. Anastasia stepped away from death row and into a new life. The legend of his escape infuriated the police, as the case against him completely collapsed and he never faced further consequences for that particular murder. Consequently, Anastasia instantly became a celebrity within the New York underworld. Everyone spoke of Albert Anastasia, the man who evaded the electric chair. Though seemingly impossible, he had achieved it.

However, once Luciano put Anastasia in charge of the alcohol and booze operations, the situation took a dark turn. The bodies began to pile up, causing profits to dwindle. In response, Luciano devised a plan and reassured his men that there was plenty for everyone to benefit from.

In order to maintain transparency, he established the Commission. Luciano convened a meeting where he distributed territories among members of his organization, giving Anastasia a significant portion. This initial gathering marked the beginning of what came to be known as 'organized crime'. Luciano's goal was to bring these gangs under his control and transform the enterprise into a potentially legitimate operation, with an unimaginable wealth potential. However, some of the older bosses opposed the idea vehemently, expressing their dissatisfaction during the first meeting. Consequently, it became clear that Luciano needed to eliminate two mob bosses, including Joe Masseria, who was considered the supreme boss of all bosses.

Anastasia, along with three other men hired by Luciano, was assigned to go to a restaurant where Masseria would be having lunch. While Luciano excused himself to use the bathroom, the men emerged from the kitchen and started shooting at Joe, hitting him six times in the chest and face. Although Masseria was riddled with bullets, he made an attempt to stand but was ultimately overwhelmed and collapsed to the floor, resulting in his death.

Next up was Salvatore Maranzano, who proved to be a much easier target. With Anastasia by his side, Luciano now had a clear path to set his plan in motion. He made the decision to reorganize the major New York families, to a certain extent, with the remaining twenty-four families. The goal was for each family to integrate and pursue legitimate business opportunities. However, the need for elimination still existed. They realized the necessity for a specialized group of hitmen to enforce the newly established rules, which later became known as "Murder Incorporated".

This group of individuals had the ability to collaborate and fulfill any requirements presented by the syndicate. Comprised of both Italians and Jews, this group of hitmen was recognized as one of the most formidable assemblages in existence. However, even they operated under strict guidelines: bosses, policemen, judges, and civilians were strictly off-limits when it came to their assassination orders in the majority of cases.

Although Albert Anastasia was a violent and ruthless individual, he also had a family. He was married to a woman 15 years younger than him. Surprisingly, he would leave for work at 8 AM and return home at 5:00 PM, dedicating time to be with his family and fulfill his role as a responsible father and husband. However, during his working hours, he predominantly engaged in acts of violence, torture, and killings. Astonishingly, he took great pleasure in his work.

Problems loomed ahead for the Commission as they became aware of Attorney General Thomas

Dewey's relentless pursuit. However, Anastasia refused to tolerate this situation. Despite the Commission's prohibition on killing politicians, Anastasia was unwilling to abide by that rule. Determined, he decided to monitor Dewey's residence on 5th Avenue, using the guise of pushing a baby carriage to avoid attracting attention. An audacious plan, as only Anastasia was bold enough to consider executing it. Unlike the Commission, Anastasia failed to grasp the broader implications of his actions. If Dewey were to be assassinated, it would undoubtedly result in immense pressure being placed on the top-tier mobsters in New York City at the time, both from local authorities and dangerously relentless federal marshals. The consequences would be catastrophic.

Before Anastasia had a chance to execute his plan, Thomas Dewey and his team apprehended Luciano in June 1936 for overseeing a prostitution ring. Luciano, the mastermind behind the Italian mob, received a 30-year prison sentence. With Luciano incarcerated, Anastasia aligned himself with Frank Costello, a prominent New York boss. However, this alliance created enmity between Carlo Gambino and Vincent Mangano, the underboss, as well as his brother Phillip Mangano.

At this particular moment, animosity towards Anastasia was widespread among the group, fueled by their discontent over his unauthorized operations for Luciano and Costello. Vito Genovese, seizing this opportunity, decided to intervene and ordered a hit on Frank Costello. However, the attempt was unsuccessful, only resulting in minor injuries, but it effectively removed Costello from the equation, allowing them to solely focus on targeting Anastasia, the infamous executioner. Three days after Costello's injury, Anastasia found himself in a barbershop, reclining in the chair while receiving a shave.

Boss Angel was in a taxi, just three blocks away from the destination. However, due to the traffic, he was running ten minutes late. Frustrated, he continuously urged the taxi driver to go faster, demanding a quicker pace. The driver explained that the current speed was the maximum allowed in the city. Filled with worry, Boss Angel decided to exit the taxi and sprint towards the barbershop. The twirling barber pole indicated its location, and he was a mere 50 yards away when suddenly, eleven shots rang out. It was too late. As he approached, Boss Angel witnessed four men fleeing the scene, hopping into a car and speeding away. Realizing the hopelessness of the situation, he hesitated to enter, knowing he had lost. Nonetheless, he stepped inside, and beheld Albert Anastasia sprawled on the floor next to the barber chair, shirtless, bearing numerous gunshot wounds, likely a minimum of ten. Initially, a fleeting wave of remorse washed over Boss Angel, but it quickly dissipated. After all, he knew Anastasia as the infamous "Lord High Executioner," responsible for over 100 hits. Despite the failure of his own attempt, he took solace in knowing that he had given his utmost effort. A victory suit would not mark this day, but somehow, in some way, a sense of triumph still lingered within him.

Chapter Four
Malcolm X

Boss Angel sits at what used to be his favorite restaurant on federal hill, Camille's Roman garden. All the men from the family would take their wives on Saturday nights and enjoy some of the best food on the East Coast. Tonight, Boss Angel is solo waiting and wondering what the mission will be and most important who will deliver it and assist!

Suddenly, from around the corner of the bar, JB walks in dressed in 1960s attire. JB says, "Don't even try to guess the era of this mission because you will fail." This is the story of the honorable and fearless Malcolm X. Born Malcolm Little on May 19, 1925, in Omaha, Nebraska, he is widely regarded as one of the most influential figures in the civil rights movement of the 1960s. His life story is characterized by transformation, activism, and a profound dedication to empowering the Black community.

Malcolm X's early life was shaped by racial discrimination and violence. His parents, Earl and Louise Little, were active supporters of Marcus Garvey's Universal Negro Improvement Association, which advocated for Black self-reliance. When Malcolm was young, his family faced threats from the Ku Klux Klan, forcing them to relocate to Lansing, Michigan.

Tragedy struck at an early age when Malcolm's father was killed by white supremacists, and his mother was subsequently institutionalized. He and his siblings were separated and placed in various foster homes. These experiences deeply influenced Malcolm's perception of systemic racism and fueled his desire for radical change.

JB, after what happened to him in his childhood, it would have been impossible to avoid racism, which back then was a more powerful force to contend with.

You're right, boss Angel, Malcolm X was a good person who tried to help his fellow man but carried the weight of the tragedies inflicted upon his family by the white man.

In his twenties, Malcolm engaged in criminal activities and was eventually sentenced to prison in 1946. It was during his time behind bars, he had a transformative experience that would alter the course of his life. It was in prison that he discovered the Nation of Islam (NOI), a religious movement advocating for the upliftment of African Americans. Influenced by NOI leader Elijah Muhammad, Malcolm converted to Islam, adopting the name Malcolm X to signify his lost African heritage.

He served a total of seven years in which he spent studying NOI and spending most of his time praising Elijah Mohammed!

Following his release from prison in 1952, Malcolm X became an influential figure within the Nation of Islam. He quickly rose through the ranks and became one of its most dynamic speakers and recruiters. Malcolm's Audience grew with tremendous followers, the venue each sermon continues to grow intensely!

Fiery and uncompromising speeches garnered attention and attracted a large following, throughout the US as he advocated for racial separatism, self-defense, and the empowerment of Black communities.

However, in 1964, Malcolm X had a transformative experience during his pilgrimage to

Mecca. Witnessing Muslims of various races and ethnicities peacefully coexisting shattered his previous beliefs about racial divisions. He returned to the United States with a newfound perspective on unity and cooperation among all races, challenging some of the Nation of Islam's teachings.

The years following his departure from the Nation of Islam were marked by intense activism and advocacy for human rights. Malcolm founded the Muslim Mosque, Inc. and the Organization of Afro-American Unity, focusing on international civil rights struggles and pursuing political avenues to address racial injustice.

This knowledge begins to turn Malcolm X against the laws of Mohammed, and he found out things about him such as forcing children of the mothers and the mothers themselves into having sexual activities and also having children with the mothers and the daughters!

On February 21, 1965, Malcolm X was scheduled to speech at the Audubon Ballroom in New York City by members associated with the Nation of Islam.

So, Boss Angel this is a difficult mission, and the expectations are low for you to make a save for Malcolm.

Listen JB I'm already developing a plan, do you remember when I met Muhammad Ali and Jim Brown together with Malcolm X and Sam Cooke?

Yes actually that was on February 15, 1965 the night the hearing of his eviction on the home and when his home was set on fire and burned to the ground. The home was owned by Elijah Mohammed. He wanted Malcolm X and his family to leave and Malcolm refused to go.

The Audubon speech was one of the reasons Muhammad Ali, Jim Brown and Sam Cooke all came together to support Malcolm on the eviction of his family's home.

Boss Angel tell me what is the plan?

If we can go back to the day before and give me enough time, I can convince Ali, Jim Brown and Sam to interfere with the attempted execution. I know Ali would not use a gun he's in the same situation as me, but Jim Brown is a very heroic man and I know he carries weapons he has a carry permit.

Boss Angel you have to realize this could end up being a huge mess both in 1964 and having to explain it to Achilles. Either way I'm with you regardless!

So, the two of them disappear in a mist. They arrived at the Hampton house where they will be celebrating Ali's victory over Sonny Listen. Boss Angel and JB are both dressed in 1960s attire. So, they knock on the room number and they introduced themselves as FBI agents telling them there's nothing to fear, we're here to explain the situation at hand.

Malcolm jumps up and says you're trying to tell me that there's a situation that you FBI agents are going to help us with? No, I'm sorry but we're not falling for it.

At that moment Jim Brown stands up and says give them the benefit of the doubt go ahead tell us what the situation is. Ali agreed and said go ahead talk.

Boss Angel tells them we have wiretapped Your home and have recorded conversations from Betty Shabazz saying that your husband is as good as dead. But that's not all, we've also recorded

Elijah Mohammed stating that you will be shot dead at the Audubon Theater.

Mohammed Ali jumped up and threw some jabs that Boss Angel and JB, of course not hitting them but scaring the daylights out of them saying how do you expect us to believe this!

Jim Brown says we can either cancel the speech or we can go and help protect Malcolm. None of these four men wanted to cancel a speech so Jim Brown opened his suitcase. He had four guns, each will have their own gun.

Boss Angel knew he was not allowed to carry a gun but being with the company that he was with, he wasn't about to turn it down, so he took a 357 magnum. Of course, JB chickened out. Malcolm X refused to carry a gun, but Sam Cooke took one and even Ali.

The speech at the Autobahn was only a couple hours away but it looked like a no-win situation.

We will all just have to do the best that we can to protect Malcolm! As a large crowd begin to enter the theater, Ali sat in the back with Jim Brown. Sam Cooke and Boss Angel are standing near the side stairs to the stage waiting for Malcom to appear.

Out comes Malcolm X to an astounding round of applause. Only moments into his speech two men start to argue with each other taking away the attention from Malcolm. Ali and Jim see two other men stand up reaching into their overcoats.

They immediately attacked, threw them to the ground and took the guns away from them. Boss Angel grabbed a man who pulled out a sawed-off shotgun from his trench coat. Boss Angel grabbed his neck until he was unconscious.

Meanwhile there was one more man who pulled out a revolver. Sam Cooke was all over him wrestling the gun away from him! Mission totally accomplished and no one was hurt, especially Malcolm!

Boss Angel's save of Malcolm X created tremendous speech, books, and teachings that continue to inspire generations of activists fighting for racial equality, self-determination, and social justice.

Malcolm X's story reflects a journey of personal and ideological transformation, shifting from an advocate of racial separatism to a proponent of interracial cooperation, unity, and the ongoing struggle for justice.

His dedication to empowering marginalized communities and challenging oppressive systems has secured his place as a symbol of resistance and an icon of the fight against racial injustice.

Chapter Five
Legs Diamond

Boss Angel awaits his instructions for the next mission when Maggie walks in, dressed like a gangster! She's wearing a black double-breasted pinstripe suit with black and white shoes, and a white ribbon around her black fedora hat. It looks like the only thing missing is the Thompson machine gun!

She sits down at the bar and has a drink. "Well, what do you think? Could I pass as one of your crew members?"

"You look marvelous, Maggie, but you don't ever want to be part of my crew, sister," Boss Angel replies. "So, according to your outfit, it looks like I'll be doing some time travel?"

"Yes, 1931."

Boss Angel and Maggie are now at the front entrance of the Copacabana nightclub in search of their mission: Legs Diamond, who Maggie doesn't need to explain. To their surprise, they see him bartending, dressed handsomely and looking very dapper. They approach the bar and listen to the dialogue between Legs Diamond and another gentleman named Dutch Schultz. They were talking about the fabulous dancers they have here at the Copacabana. How well trained they are, thanks to him. Dutch asks, "What do you mean, what did you do to make them fabulous?"

"Well, I have been a dance instructor for 25 years," replies Legs Diamond. His eyes open wide, and then he pauses.

Boss Angel felt someone tap him on the back. To his surprise, it was his Angel pal JB. Boss Angel stood up and gave him a big hug. JB said, "I'm here to give you your mission, but let's move to a booth where we can talk." Maggie gave JB a hug and slid into the booth with them.

"Do you see those two fine-looking gentlemen you were sitting with at the bar?" JB asked.

"Yes, they look like real nice guys. Who are they?" Boss Angel replied.

"The Italian with the black hair is Legs Diamond," Maggie explained. "When he was alive, he was Arnold Rothstein's underboss. He was known for a couple of things. One, his double pearl-handled quick six-shooter ability. And the other?"

"Simply surviving being shot four times, even though he was only expected to survive three," JB added.

The other one is Dutch Schultz, known for his violent temper! He had ties to the Jewish boss Meyer Lansky, ties such as murder, and he was great with a knife! So, it's Legs Diamond who is the mission? Yes, it is, buddy boy. That's kind of strange, they were only talking about dancing, from what I heard.

JB says, "Yes, as a matter of fact, Boss Angel, rumor has it, you can cut up a pretty good rug yourself."

Boss Angel tells JB, "Keep that one to yourself, will you!"

As the conversations continued in the other booth, Legs and the Dutchman spoke about him being able to teach men how to dance. Legs laughed at him and said, "In all my years of training, I never even had a man approach me to learn how to dance. But now that I think about it, I think we might be able to work something out. If we can be discreet, it will save embarrassment while you learn, Dutch."

The very next afternoon, Dutch meets Legs at the Copacabana. Maggie, JB, and Boss Angel appear and sit in a VIP booth at the far end of the club. JB and Maggie continue to take turns explaining more about the mission and delving deeper into each of their characters.

Maggie says, "The Copacabana may just be one of the most famous nightclubs ever! It's a favorite of Hollywood celebrities, athletes, and even mobsters! Frank Costello was one of the early partners, and Joe Gallo ran the joint until 1972. It has always been the place to be. It appeared in movies like Goodfellas, Raging Bull, and even Carlito's Way. There's even a song named after it!

Yes, the one by Barry Manilow, 'Copacabana.' A New York City institution, it has cemented itself as a must-visit because there's never been anything quite like it. There was more dancing at the Copacabana than at all the other clubs in New York combined."

Gentlemen prepare to be entertained! As a man named Arnold Rothstein approaches the booth and introduces himself, "I'm Arnold Rothstein." Just as Legs walks toward the men's room, Rothstein compliments him, saying, "I was amazed by the balance you showed with your moves on the dance floor yesterday! Would you like a job dancing or teaching for me?"

Dutch has a great idea. He tells Rothstein to give them a moment to discuss it. Dutch convinces Legs, "It will be a way for you to meet girls, and this is a way for us to move in on Arnold Rothstein and take over the club."

Legs responds, "It does sound like an offer we can't refuse!"

The footwork of Legs Diamond already had Rothstein amazed, especially when it comes to tap dancing. These teachings continue for a few weeks. Boss Angel is asked by Rothstein what he thinks, based on what he's seen on the dance floor. Boss Angel offers his opinion, saying, "By doing some numbers with the girls, you'll do just fine."

That evening was Friday night, a very busy evening, but Legs made a terrible mistake the following day. He was walking by the hotel two blocks away and looked in the window. He saw some of the men who worked at the Copa for Rothstein buying items from the showcase, such as cigars, cigarette lighters, wallets, and even cufflinks. What caught his attention was that they were all just signing Arnold Rothstein's name.

Legs figured that since he was now working for Rothstein, he could be a part of the crew by picking items from the showcase himself and just signing Rothstein's name!

Legs did this for a few days straight until one day, while purchasing items at the hotel showcases.

Suddenly, two of Rothstein's men approached him from behind and instructed, "Come with us. Mr. Rothstein wants to see you!" Reluctantly, Legs followed them until he stood in front of Rothstein, fully aware that he had been caught. But Legs decided to take another angle.

When Rothstein began to speak, Legs interrupted him and explained that the only reason he had been taking items from the downstairs commissary was that he wanted to meet Rothstein and prove that he's not just a dancer. He boldly stated that he should be Rothstein's bodyguard instead of relying on the two goons present. In that tense moment, both goons reached for their guns, but Legs swiftly drew his own six-shooters and had them covered. "See, Mr. Rothstein, they're not capable of protecting you, but I am," Legs asserted.

In that decisive moment, Arnold Rothstein hired Legs Diamond as his official bodyguard.

Here's where everything changed: Legs Diamond grew strong working for Rothstein, so he decided to buy the Copacabana. Boss Angel also continued to work and was as good as Legs. One night, Boss Angel absolutely wowed the crowd, including Legs Diamond! At this point, JB needs to catch up with Boss Angel and explain the rest of the mission. There are many nights similar to the first night and the crowd goes wild for Boss Angel.

One night, Charles "Lucky" Luciano entered the club with Dutch Schultz, appearing to attempt a shakedown. And it was indeed a shakedown! Boss Angel witnessed the manager of the Copacabana handing them a stack of money while they sat in a VIP booth. Boss Angel's typical reaction would be to reach for his nickel-plated .38. However, since he had been disarmed, Boss Angel approached them in the booth and said, "You can't do this to me, I'm Legs Diamond."

Luciano started laughing hysterically. He exclaimed, "What kind of a crazy name is that? You must have some pretty sexy legs there, boy, we saw you up there." Schultz remained silent, but Legs continued, saying, "I am not going to allow you to take money from this establishment. I don't care who you are, I'm not afraid of anybody. If I were you gentlemen, I would leave and never come back." With that, they appeared to walk away, and it was nice talking to them.

At that moment, shots rang out from across the club. Legs sprang into action, diving on top of Charlie "Lucky" Luciano. The bullet narrowly missed Luciano and struck Dutch Schultz twice in the torso and once in the head. Legs himself was wounded in the shoulder and stomach. Knowing that Schultz was dead, Legs drove himself to the hospital where he stayed for a few days before returning to the Copa.

Legs realized that it was Rothstein who had sent Luciano out of fear for his own life. Not even two weeks had passed, and things had already calmed down. While he healed, Legs was unable to do much, but he remained determined to seek revenge and was confident about breaking even. Legs Diamond was truly courageous!

Once back at the Copa, Charlie and his men approached Legs. "It appears you have a lot of balls, young man," Charlie said. "I could use someone like you in my syndicate."

Legs Diamond replied firmly, "There is only one thing I'm interested in right now, and that's tap dancing and a little bit of swing. If your syndicate has either one of those in its repertoire, then I'll consider it. Otherwise, I'm not going to end up like this dead moron on the floor! Thanks, but no thanks! I'd much rather be dancing!"

Legs Diamond proved himself more than once after his first score was retrieved. Instead of Luciano, Legs ended up working for Arnold Rothstein in the rackets. In the eyes of Boss Angel, Legs didn't have much of a choice.

It wasn't long before Lucky wanted revenge against Legs for joining one of his enemies, Arnold Rothstein! On three different occasions, attempts were made on Legs. The second attempt involved a shotgun blast, but once again, Legs managed to survive and heal.

Some may say it's a shame that Dutch Schultz didn't have his day in court, but his actions at the Copa that day proved there was no need for a second chance! Speaking of a second chance, there was even a fourth attempt on Legs, this time set up by his girlfriend. She tipped off men connected to Luciano! Legs always carried two pearl-handled nickel-plated .38 revolvers. While asleep in her apartment, two men entered, but when Legs woke up and reached for his guns, they were gone. Legs had convinced most people that he was immortal. Even as he lay on the bed, screaming at the killers, "What's wrong with you guys? You can't kill me, I'm Legs Diamond!" One man ran out in fear, but the other shot Legs three times in the head. Boss Angel arrived just a minute too late! He will have some explaining to do to Achilles. Although deep down, Boss Angel already knew. Some people you just can't save.

Chapter Six
Humphrey Bogart

JB comes walking into the Biltmore Hotel lounge wearing a full-length raincoat tied at the waist. He moves the dark round fedora tilted to the left side of his face. He walks over to Boss Angel, who is facing sideways, so he doesn't really see him coming. As he sneaks up on Boss Angel, he says, "It would have been impossible to guess at this moment in 1939 that Humphrey Bogart, who was playing Doctor X in this really awful horror movie, would eventually become the most iconic actor in the history of cinema."

JB, I was wondering when we were going to do the Bogart save? This will certainly be one that will be really exciting! I mean, just seeing Humphrey Bogart would be a thrill for me, JB.

By this point, Bogart had already made something like 40 films, most as a contract player for Warner Brothers. He was never a leading man at this point. Warner cast him almost exclusively as a villain, usually in the gangster pictures that flourished in the 1930s.

Bogart was a constant presence in that decade, but a minor one. But in the 1940s, everything changed. It started with this movie, High

Sierra, and the leading role that Bogart's contemporary, George Raft, turned down because he was tired of being typecast as a gangster. The character was Mad Dog Roy Earle, a thief who has just been let out of jail and agrees to do one last job.

I see him as a kind of coda on the fading gangster era, and maybe it's because he played so many of these characters.

Bogart lends the perfect world weariness to a story that seems fated to end in tragedy. Earl's hardened but sympathetic, or at least you get the sense that he wants to believe there's something sympathetic in himself.

High Sierra was a hit, and it began a new phase in Bogart's career. He knew then what it was all about. That same year, he helped Hollywood say goodbye to the '30s gangster picture! Bogart introduced the world to film noir with The Maltese Falcon. This wasn't the first of Bogart's truly iconic roles. Private detective Sam Spade, John Huston's directorial debut, was another part turned down by George Raft. The character of a hard-boiled, wise-cracking PI is archetypal and thrilling to watch.

Bogart created the character for the movies with the help of Huston's script from the novel. His inspired direction of Bogie as the tough guy, again, this time on the other side of the law. In Sam Spade, he finds another layer of vulnerability, especially in the astonishing final minutes. "You never understand me," he says, "but I'll try once, and then give it up."

The alert genius wasn't in his range as an actor. He didn't have much but a star with the golden era. He wasn't allowed anywhere. What Bogart lacked in variety, he made up for in depth. He went inward and took the type he was so well known for as a cynical, bruised, world-weary, but still hopeful man.

A year after The Maltese Falcon in 1942, he starred in Casablanca, and no one could have pulled off Rick Blaine better than Bogie. This was a tricky part. The first half hour of the movie calls for him to be cold, bitter, and generally unlikable. This was meant for Bogie to distance himself from the character, yet somehow he draws us in because he brings a naturalism to the part that enlivens the otherwise cliché elements of the story. It isn't just cynicism, it's a shield on the topmost layer concealing how Bogart allows us into this pain through his eyes without any action at all. He's totally transparent to the viewer, so that even the slightest twitch in his face feels like an earthquake. With Casablanca, Bogart added "romantic lead" to his repertoire, co-staring Ingrid Bergman. From there he built on his romantic lead status with four films co-staring his future wife, Lauren Bacall.

Bogart wasn't the tall, handsome leading man like Cary Grant. His face was lined with years of hard drinking, yet there's something attractive about a man whose coolness betrays an inner reservoir of feeling. In the Big Sleep, he brings that romantic chemistry.

But in another classic, The Private Eye Philip Marlowe, Boss Angel is a testament to Bogart's charisma under the direction of Howard Hawks. This is a story that is famously incomprehensible, yet still compulsively watchable. I will let you have it.

The Treasure of the Sierra Madre finds another gear for Bogie. He plays a man prospecting for gold with two others, and they strike it rich. But greed and paranoia tear them apart. This was a new kind of role for Bogart, but it's also a further exploration of the character he had been developing in Casablanca and his Bacall films. The vulnerability he conceals under his tough guy shell emerges as love or compassion in The Treasure of the Sierra Madre. What's inside him eventually curdles and develops into madness and rage as his eyes burn with it. "Go ahead, brother sweet brother," he says in his best Bogie imitation voice. "You love her, and she's deceived you! You hate her patronizing attitude. She looks down on you. She's impressed with celebrity. She wants to get rid of you. Squeeze harder, squeeze harder. It's wonderful to feel your throat crush."

Even more disturbing was Director Nicholas Ray's in A Lonely Place, where Bogart plays a washed-up, boozy screenwriter who is wrongly accused of murder. You can see how the moral backbone of characters like Rick Blaine, Sam Spade, and Philip Marlowe kept him afloat, and how hope provided stability. Lose that, and the cynicism starts to look a lot like sociopathy, and self-doubt leads to self-hatred, finally becoming dangerous. Bogart knew, perhaps from experience, how easy it is to fall on either side of the coin.

Bogart turned in more great performances in the 50s, in movies like The African Queen. This is when he truly became a legend.

In 1957, at the age of 57, he died of esophageal cancer. Throughout his life, he had the fortune to be involved with great projects and great directors, but they also had the fortune to be involved with Humphrey Bogart. He elevated and deepened all of his films, and he took his craft seriously.

OK Boss Angel, I know by now you've figured out a way to save Humphrey Bogart! I failed to mention that back in 1950, give or take a year or two, Humphrey Bogart formed the Rat Pack, which ended up being a group of friends including Sammy Davis, Joey Lewis, Peter Lawford, Dean Martin, and Frank Sinatra.

Bogie was the ringleader, and they stuck together like glue. There has never been a group of men with more talent than the Rat Pack! They made "Ocean's Eleven," a famous Las Vegas movie, and put on their own show of comedy and song that was loved worldwide. Unfortunately, as I mentioned earlier, Bogie developed cancer, and it wasn't long before it took him from us. So, have you figured out what we can do to save him? Don't forget, Boss Angel, he has already passed, so this will not be easy.

I already have an idea, JB. I suggest we go back in time to the movie set of Casablanca.

OK, Boss Angel, the movie was on January 23rd, 1943. We'll go there and act as extras. No one will know who we are or why we're there, as long as we put on the correct wardrobe. Now, what's your plan once we arrive, Boss Angel?

Our mission will be to convince Bogart that he must stop smoking and drinking alcohol.

Oh, really? That's kind of a long shot, don't you think?

Do you have any serum left from the last mission?

Sorry, Boss Angel. That's not going to work. It's too long between his death!

JB why don't you try coming up with an idea?

Come on think of something!

OK, I have an idea. Obviously, Lauren Bacall will be there, and if we can influence her enough to make Bogart quit, even if we have to reveal what lies ahead, we will. Well, we have enough angles to use here, so let's gather the wardrobes and head back to 1943.

Boss Angel and JB find themselves on the set of Casablanca. As they walk in, they spot Sam, the piano player, warming up. They are both astonished by the set and the number of people present.

JB, it appears they are getting ready to begin shooting. They're probably just waiting for Ingrid Bergman and Bogie. JB, that gives me an idea. How about if I approach his fiancé, Lauren Bacall and just be direct? Don't forget, she's madly in love with him, JB, and would probably do anything to help out.

JB answers, "I thought you were going to work your way in there. What happened to that idea?"

"No, I think it'll be better if I just approach her right off the bat. This really should be taken more seriously than just beating around the bush."

OK, well, don't look now, but she just walked through the front door, and the problem is she's with Bogie.

JB, they're both heading towards the bar. I think I'll go over there and start small talk.

OK, go ahead. Good luck. I'll keep an eye on things from this end. Bogie and Bacall are casually sipping on a martini, with Bogie holding a cigarette in his mouth. Sam softly plays a jazz tune on the piano. After a few minutes, Ingrid Bergman appears from makeup and Bogie excuses himself and heads to the men's room because it seems that shooting is about to begin soon.

Boss Angel taps Lauren Bacall on the shoulder. "Hello there, how are you?"

"Well, I'm Lauren Bacall, who are you?"
"They call me Gino, Gino Suraci."
"So, Gino, what can I do for you?"
"Well, I'm going to have to make this quick. Bogie has cancer caused by smoking and drinking alcohol. He has an opportunity to cure it only if he quits both smoking and drinking."

Lauren asks, "Who are you and where are you from, and how do you know these things? And why should I believe you?"

"If I told you I was an Angel, and I came here specifically to help Bogie, would you believe me?"

"Well, whether or not I believe you, I am desperate to have him quit both drinking and smoking. We have had arguments and it has almost torn us apart."

"Lauren, there's one main element that could cure everything, and that is love. If you threaten him with the loss of your love, I can guarantee he will obey."

Lauren says, "Well, then it's obvious you don't know Humphrey Bogart, but there's something about you, Gino."

"No, Lauren, my name is Boss Angel, and I work for Achilles, the Archangel!"

"Well, whoever you are, whoever you work for, wherever you came from, I think you have ignited something inside of me, and I will do everything I can to make it work!"

"I am so proud of you, Lauren, and I've just met you. But look out, here comes Bogie. Good luck now, Lauren. I have confidence in your confidence that you will not let him down. So, enjoy making the movie."

Boss Angel bends over and gives Lauren a nice, respectful hug, then walks away to the other side of the building. "JB, I think that did the trick. I think she's going to help him make his cancer disappear."

"JB, how are we going to know if we're successful or not?"

"Only time will tell, my Boss Angel. Only time will tell."

Chapter Seven
Jimi Hendrix

Boss Angel sits at the bar inside the Biltmore Hotel, waiting for one of his Angel assistants to deliver him the next mission. Moments later, Maggie comes walking in with a minidress full of psychedelic colors, knee-high boots, and a black Afro wig, complete with a bandana! Boss Angel tells her she looks like she's ready for Woodstock.

"Maggie, why do you always have to play the role? You're always trying to make me guess!" he says.

"Well, you're yet to get one correct," she replies.

"It kind of hurts my feelings, you know. I'm sorry, Maggie. I get a little jittery before each of these missions, so please accept my apology."

"I accept, though you were really close when you said Woodstock!"

"Alright, Maggie. I'll take a guess. Was it Sly and the Family Stone?"

Close but no cigar. It was Jimi Hendrix, the legendary guitarist, widely regarded as one of the most innovative and influential musicians in the history of rock music. His electrifying performances and unparalleled guitar skills revolutionized the world. He frequently incorporated themes of peace into his songs, becoming an emblematic figure of the anti-war movement during the turbulent times of the 1960s. At the height of his fame, he headlined Woodstock in 1969.

Today, we are celebrating and honoring the greatest guitarist in the world by listing his accomplishments. We are also going to explore how his career as a rock star began and reflect on the unfortunate events surrounding his untimely death. Maggie that's a great way to honor such a great person, he was another one of those young musicians who died at a young age, what a shame Maggie!

Jimi Hendrix was originally born as Johnny Allen Hendrix to a teenage mother and a father who served in the army. Both of his parents possessed musical abilities, particularly in dance. However, due to disputes between his parents, Jimi's name was legally changed to James Marshall Hendrix. Everyone knew him by the nickname Jimi, spelled Jimi, from the day he was born on November 27th, 1942, in Seattle, WA. He had a birthday numerology of the number 27, which was also the age he would be when he passed away. Jimi became another famous celebrity member of the infamous 27 club.

Jimi's brother, Leon Hendricks, shares that Jimi was so fascinated by the radio that he took a screwdriver and dismantled it, saying, "I was looking for music." Jimi's aunt lent him five dollars to buy a second-hand guitar. Since it was a right-handed guitar, he had to turn it upside down to play it. Leon recalls that Jimi could play really fast even at the age of 13, performing songs by Chuck Berry, Little Richard, and Elvis.

By the time he turned 18, Jimi was already a musical prodigy. However, he had lost interest in high school and became a dropout. On May 2nd, 1961 he seemed to have been caught up in a rift between the police, who allegedly caught him riding in a stolen vehicle. FBI records filed upon Jimi's arrest noted that the next day Jimi would be offered either a two-year prison sentence or take enlistment in the US army. The latter is the decision he went with. He was assigned to be a paratrooper at the 101st airborne division. He was stationed in the Deep South in Fort Campbell.

Jimi Hendrix, the stage name he would later adopt on the advice of his big media manager, raises questions about whether the army has been scouting individuals since birth to shape their lives. It is worth noting that Jimi was reportedly rebellious during his time in the army. Nevertheless, he remained true to his passion for music and continued playing the guitar. Though signed up for three years of service, Jimi's ankle injury during a parachute jump hastened his departure from active duty, resulting in an honorable discharge.

In 1962, Jimi Hendrix gladly accepted his discharge, even though he lacked the funds to return home to Seattle. Instead, he relocated to nearby Nashville, TN, with Billy Cox, where they formed the band 'King Casuals' and became the house band at the club Del Morocco. Despite this opportunity, 'King Casuals' did not offer Jimi the exposure or financial security he desired. Consequently, he left the band and joined the chitlin circuit. Interestingly, the tenure of 'King Casuals' was short-lived.

It's noteworthy that during Jimi's career, he had the privilege of sharing the stage with numerous iconic artists such as Ella Fitzgerald, The Jackson 5, Aretha Franklin, Billie Holiday, Etta James, B.B. King, Otis Redding, Little Richard, Tina Turner, The Isley Brothers, Muddy Waters to name a few of the legends in music history during 1962 to 1965.

Jimi Hendrix played with at least two dozen bands and performed in over 100 cities. During those years, he rarely took on the role of front man for a band. In 1965, he made his first-ever TV appearance alongside Buddy and Stacy, a duo of Long Island singers, in Nashville.

He later joined Junior Walker and the All Stars for a performance of their top ten hit, 'Shotgun'. This marked one of the final instances where Hendrix would be in the shadows of other bandleaders. Inspired by Butch Snipes and Alfonso Baby Boo, Jimi began incorporating techniques like playing the guitar strings with his teeth. His style continued to evolve, and his comfort with playing blues served as a precursor to his later groovy and over-the-top stage antics.

By 1965, Jimi Hendrix had grown tired of the chitlin circuit and relocated to Harlem in New York City. There, he struck out on his own while still working as a sideman. He recorded with The Isley Brothers and toured with Little Richard. It's worth mentioning that The Beatles had already covered songs by The Isley Brothers, and other artists had also been performing renditions of their tracks Including

Tall Sally by Little Richard. This was the first crossover into an international rock circuit.

Jimi Hendrix would later become friends with The Beatles and worked steadily in New York City as a session player. During this period, he referred to himself as Jimmy James. He joined Curtis Knight for a performance at the Club Cheetah between May 12th and May 25th, 1966. It is worth noting that Jimi Hendrix also played with Keith Richards, a founding member of The Rolling Stones, who was a rival group to The Beatles from the UK.

In May 1966, while in New York, Jimi Hendrix met Linda Keith, who was deeply impressed by his performances. Linda borrowed The Rolling Stones' white Stratocaster guitar and gave it to Jimi on an indefinite loan. She also supposedly introduced him to LSD, which is captured in his films. It's important to mention that at that time, LSD was still legal, although it would soon be outlawed.

Suspicious in terms of being scouted by the industry in 1966, Linda Keith inspired Jimi to form his own band, Jimmy James and the Blue Flames. It was folk singer Richie Havens who recommended and suggested that Jimi Hendrix try his luck at the downtown club café, where Bob Dylan first performed. When he arrived in New York in 1961, Jimi was a huge fan of Bob Dylan, as evident in his later cover versions of Dylan's songs. The historic café immediately offered Jimi a residency spot in Greenwich Village, New York City, allowing him to develop his own audience after years of conforming to uniforms, rules, and enduring frequent ridicule in the chitlin circuit.

Jimi's repertoire included soul covers like "In the Midnight Hour" and "Knock on Wood," as well as crowd-pleasers such as "Hey Joe" and "Like a Rolling Stone." Sometimes, they even performed a 20-minute rendition of "Summertime." Jimi also learned a murder ballad called "Hey Joe," which had captivated him when he first heard it on a nearby jukebox.

'Hey Joe' had been done before, but Jimi loved this new slow version and worked it into his set. Linda Keith was impressed by Jimi's new band and later brought Chaz Chandler, the bassist for another famous UK band, The Animals. You'll probably remember The Animals from their single "House of the Rising Sun," which Jimi was already covering in his sets, so he must have been genuinely happy to meet Chaz Chandler.

At this point, Jimi was looking to begin managing and producing and was searching for someone to help produce "Hey Joe." On July 5th, 1966, Linda invited Chaz to an afternoon set at the Cafe War. Jimi began his set with that very song, "Hey Joe." It's also known that Linda Keith was essentially flirting with Jimi, and after he was scouted, she ghosted him and pretended to have nothing more to do with him. She was paid to be an instigator and move paperwork along, using her beauty to sell the image of sex, drugs, and rock'n'roll to a naive and vulnerable Jimi Hendrix! Linda Keith even stated, "I've seen good guitar players before, like James Marshall (Jimi's birth name) and Keith Richards of The Rolling Stones, who broke up with Linda Keith due to her closeness with Jimi Hendrix." He was likely playing along, knowing that his name and reputation were being used in the industry as a name drop and gear kit for grooming new artists.

The guitar that Keith Richards donated to Jimi Hendrix via Linda was a 1964 Fender Stratocaster with an Olympic white finish. It's no secret that Jim recorded all his "Experience" albums at the Olympic Studios. Chaz Chandler, a puppet in the industry, doesn't seem like the worst character in this story. He genuinely seemed to have an interest in producing good music. Chandler recalls, "I immediately thought he was the best guitarist I'd ever seen," and he hit it off with Jimi, inviting him to try his luck in the UK.

"Maggie, it appears that he was the greatest guitarist that ever lived—a talent that will never be duplicated," says Boss Angel.
"I agree with you, Boss Angel. There will never be anyone like him again."

When the Animals' tour finished, Jimi famously didn't have a passport and was hesitant to travel to the UK. At this moment, Jimi asked Chaz if he could arrange a meeting with his idol, the legendary English rock musician Eric Clapton. It is said that Chaz Chandler was able to make this meeting happen. Chaz suggested permanently changing Jimi's first name from Jimmy to Jimi since he was already using it anyway, and Jimi agreed.

To secure a recording contract for Jimi, Chaz felt that he needed a partner who could provide the funds and the industry knowledge to launch his new protégé's career. He turned to Mike Jeffery, a gangster he knew in the industry. Despite the fact that Mike Jeffery had apparently ripped off The Animals, Chandler knew he was still under contract to Jeffery, which meant that Jeffery would have a claim to part of any money should their new producing venture be successful. Unfortunately,

Jeffery would turn out to be the worst handler of them all: a violent, money-laundering mobster who later instigated Jimi's murder.

Regardless, upon his arrival in London on the evening of September 24, 1966, Jimi Hendrix played his first-ever solo gig in the UK at the exclusive Scotch of Saint James Club in Masons Yard.

Mason's was an old art gallery where John Lennon met Yoko Ono, and it was a stone's throw from Buckingham Palace. The club at Mason's Yard was popular with The Beatles and The Rolling Stones, both of whom enjoyed the luxury of their own private tables. The Who and Stevie Wonder also spent time here.

Immediately after his first set at Mason's Yard, Jimi met Kathy Etchingham. Kathy was a hairdresser, popular DJ, and a familiar face around the city's rock scene. The pair embarked upon a two-year relationship.

The following month, Hendrix returned to the Scotch of Saint James at Mason's Yard with hired musicians Mitch Mitchell and Noel Redding, who together formed the Jimi Hendrix Experience. It was at this venue that the trio performed their UK debut on the evening of October 1, 1966.

Jimi Hendrix was finally invited to watch cream starring, Eric Clapton, perform The London Howlin Wolf Session. Jimi Hendrix got invited and jammed with Eric Clapton and afterwards, Eric

Clapton wandered over to Chandler and said you never told me he was that fucking good! Despite their guitar duo Eric Clapton and Jimi Hendrix became firm friends on the 11th of October 1966.

Mike Jeffery and Chaz Chandler arranged a meeting with Hendricks and Mitchell at the offices of their company on Gerrard Street in London for the contract and Jimi Hendrix and the experience signed. At the meeting was a production deal whereby Mike Jeffery and Chaz Chandler would be record producers. On the 23rd of October 1966, Chaz Chandler brought Jimi Hendrix, Mitch Mitchell and Noel Redding to Delane Lee studios for the Jimi Hendrix Experience's very first recording of 'Hey Joe'. It was November 25th

1966. This was the first Jimi Hendrix experience gig as a trio which would send shockwaves through Britain's rock royalty. The band wowed the crowd received many accolades from those present including John Lennon and Paul McCartney.

Their performance at the Bag O' Nails established the Jimi Hendrix Experience as a force to be reckoned with. Paul McCartney met his future wife Linda at this very same club. However, there is very little information about the exact time Jimi and Paul McCartney met. There is a conspiracy theory that Jimi actually met a Paul McCartney impersonator named Billy Shears, but regardless, if he did know the secret about The Beatles, it seems he had to keep quiet about it. Adding to the eeriness of the whole conspiracy is the fact that there are no photos of Jimi Hendrix with The Beatles!

On the internet, there is written evidence that Jimi Hendrix met every single member of The Beatles, but why are there no photos of that? Why would big media not want to commemorate the fact that the best guitar player and the best band in the world had met and were friends? Why can't we celebrate the fact that many media outlets and rock magazines were in a fury to find these photos or videos? Is the censorship of these photos and videos of Jimi Hendrix with The Beatles part of a smear campaign to destroy Jimi's legacy and make his legacy fade into obscurity? All we know is that a recording of Jimi Hendrix and John Lennon performing a cover of The Beatles' "Day Tripper" exists on vinyl and in bootleg form.

Jimi Hendrix rented the basement at 34 Montague Square in London from Ringo Starr between December 1966 and March 1967, along with his girlfriend Kathy Etchingham. While living in Ringo's basement, Jimi had an argument with Kathy and composed "The Wind Cries Mary."

34 Montague Square went on to become a famous address, with rumors of a very sexy bathroom adorned with lots of mirrors. As a result, the home has numerous connections with The Beatles. The song "Eleanor Rigby" was developed there, and later, the racy cover for John Lennon and

Yoko Ono's two Virgin albums was snapped on the premises.

The most iconic photos of Jimi Hendrix wearing an army coat were taken in front of this building, along with the photos of Jimi inside The Beatles' apartment.

Unfortunately, in March of 1967, the master Freemason Ringo apparently had no choice and no option but to evict Jimi Hendrix when the guitarist, while under the influence, splashed paint all over the walls. This story is funny and odd. Jimi Hendrix's friendship with The Beatles is one of our favorite musical connections.

The Jimi Hendrix Experience wowed the crowd at the Finsbury Astoria, where at the end of the set, Jimi carried out the ritual of setting fire to his guitar on stage for the first time. Later, he would explain the sacrifice, stating, "you sacrifice the things you love, I love my guitar." There is a lot of speculation as to why Jimi Hendrix used on-stage gimmicks. Was this his own creation or forced upon by his handlers? Hendrix's neurolinguistic marketing of this event started 27 weeks after he first arrived in London, England.

The Jimi Hendrix experience worked on all three of their studio albums, Are You Experienced, Axis Bold as Love and Electric Lady Land at the Olympic! Linda Keith invited The Jimi Hendrix

Experience to perform at number of electrifying events at the sable throughout 1967 and 1968 and with The Beatles in attendance. Jimi paid tribute to his friends with a cover of Sergeant Pepper's Lonely Hearts club band, an extraordinary gesture.

The track and album of the same name had only been released three days previously when Jimi Hendrix and the Experience headed to America, where they took the Monterey Festival by storm. Hendrix came back to London for a few shows at the Saville Theatre on August 27th, 1967, but the second concert was cancelled upon hearing of The Beatles' manager, Brian Epstein's death.

In 1968, Jimi Hendrix had the intention of making London his main base. In anticipation of his return, Jimi's partner, Kathy Etchingham, secured a flat on the top two floors of 23 Brook Street, Mayfair, minutes away from the American embassy on Grosvenor Square. Jimi Hendrix settled in, warmly describing the apartment as "my first real home of my own." A camp bed was also kept handy for the numerous musicians wishing to sleep over at Jimi and Kathy's place. George Harrison was one such guest. When Jimi Hendrix first came to 23 Brook Street, he was intrigued to discover that another musician, the German-British Baroque composer George Frederick Handel, had once lived next door. After discovering this, Jimmy went out to buy the full set of Handel's work on vinyl at his favorite record shop, the One Stop Music Shop on South Molton Street. It is possible to spot Handel's influences in Hendrix's work. Handel's 25 Brook Street Apartment has since been restored and is now open to the public.

Upon Jimi's return to London, he appeared on the BBC's LuLu show. The Hendrix Experience had one of their worst gigs ever.

On his way to New York on May 3rd, 1969, Jimi Hendrix was arrested at the Toronto airport in possession of a small amount of what they suspected to be heroin and hashish in his luggage. Mike Jeffery was on holiday in Hawaii at the time, but when they spoke on the phone, Hendrix told him that the drugs had been planted. Mike Jeffery told Hendrix not to worry about the drug charges, saying that he had everything well in hand. Some people close to Hendrix had suggested that Mike Jeffery had been responsible for planting the drugs on him. Hendrix thought that he was being overworked and made to tour all over the world without any regard to how he was feeling! He didn't like the fact that the money he was earning was supposedly going to the Bahamas and not into his own account. Jimi thought he was being treated like a kid who was incapable of handling the money he was making.

Jimi was feeling trapped by a situation that he couldn't legally escape from because he shared the same firm of lawyers with Mike Jeffery. He could tell it was a total inside job and just too much of a coincidence that there was suddenly a 34-page file from the FBI which began an investigation into Jimi

Hendrix. Following the drug charge in Toronto in 1969, declassified FBI documents show that Hendrix appeared on a list of dissident musicians' writers and artists who would be put into a detainment camp in the United states should the escalating black radicalism and violent opposition to the Vietnam War reached the point of national emergency!

The FBI's Jimi Hendrix dossier states illegal narcotics possession. Soon after this, Jimi Hendrix was distancing himself from the Experience and rehearsing with his old buddy Billy Cox on bass. The new band was to be known as Gypsy, Sun, and the Rainbows. Jimi Hendrix was due to appear at the Woodstock Festival on Sunday, August 17th, 1969, which was officially the last day of the festival. When he arrived in Bethel, NY, where the festival was held, there were torrential downpours, so he had to perform the next day as Mike Jeffery arranged with the organizers for his appearance to be delayed. On Monday, July 18th, 33 days after the fake moon landing, as most conspiracy theorists believe, the conspiracy of Woodstock was that it was a test of military exercises with large crowds. But Woodstock will be remembered as the most iconic moment in rock history. On August 18th, 1969, legendary guitarist Jimi Hendrix stepped onto the stage and embarked upon an uninterrupted set lasting over two hours.

Hendrix's electric guitar performance of the star-spangled banner has gone down in history as one of the most iconic. It was widely praised for its creativity and originality and has been hailed as a masterpiece of rock music!

In September 1969, Jimi Hendrix was recording in New York and involved with jazz producer Alan Douglas. Douglas wanted to draw Hendrix into jazz and team him up with jazz trumpeter Miles Davis in the band of Gypsies. Jimi Hendrix would record with Billy Cox on bass. Many of us truth believers insist that the Hendrix death has all the marks of a homicide.

In the weeks before his death, Hendrix indicated that he believed he would not live much longer. He is said to have remarked, "The next time

I go to Seattle will be in a pine box, and I'm not sure I will live to be 28 years old!" Three things to me about the end, one of which is, I don't know how much longer I'm going to be doing what I'm doing. Then he says, "I don't know how much longer I'm going to be moving clocks!" He knew the end was coming, and he was here for maybe four more days. Just before he died, he asked, "Have you heard about J Edgar Hoover?" We now know that Hoover ordered the Bureau to expose, disrupt, misdirect, discredit, and otherwise neutralize African Americans organizations and leaders as part of the bloody cartel pro campaign.

We also know that Hendrix was being investigated by the FBI. At the time of his death, agents had a lengthy dossier on him, along with other high-profile radicals of the civil rights, black power, and anti-war movements, some of whom died similarly abrupt and strange deaths. At the height of their influence, tactics were ruthless and highly personalized. It was all part of an attempt to stifle the spread of anti-establishment ideas. Jimi's meteoric rise to fame and his public affiliation with revolutionaries would have made him an obvious target of the Feds.

Jimi returned to London and checked into the Cumberland Hotel on the 6th of September 1970, and used the room on and off, seeing Kathy and Chaz. Jimi would go back and forth to the Cumberland Hotel over the next 12 days, using his room more as a crash pad rather than a home. His final interviews were recorded at the hotel on the 11th of September for the BBC. We know 911 is always a suspicious date, so that's disturbing.

Jimi Hendrix came to Ronnie Scotts on the night of the 16th of September 1970 and jammed with American funk band Eric Ferdinand of War. Eric was the lead singer of The Animals, and Jimi was known to hang out with the animals a lot because Chaz Chandler, his handler was the bassist of the animals. But it would be the last ever time Jimi performed live on stage, and his performance was uncharacteristically subdued.

Bobby Walason

By September 1970, Jimi Hendrix was in a new relationship with Monica Dannemann, a German artist and figure skater who was renting accommodations at the Samarkand, a self-catering apartment hotel in the heart of Noting Hill. On the 17th of September, Hendrix and Monica spent the day together visiting King's Road and the Cumberland Hotel that afternoon. While drinking tea in the garden of the Samarkand Hotel, Jimi posed for photographs, the last of which would ever be taken of him.

I think it's time Maggie let's travel to London and get a room at the Cumberland hotel because you know we only get one shot at this. Maggie agrees and beams herself and boss Angel to the Samarkand hotel in London, where they would rent a hotel room right next door to Jimi Hendrix.

Later that night, Jimmy and Monica attended a party and returned to the Samarkand Hotel sometime after 3:00 AM. The following morning, around 11:00 AM, Monica awoke to find Jimi sleeping but unresponsive. Panicked, she called for an ambulance, and left the room to go down to the office.

Maggie and Boss Angel entered the room to find Jimi covered in vomit. Boss Angel quickly grabbed a syringe and administered a shot to help him recover. Meanwhile, Maggie cleaned up Jimi, who started breathing rapidly. Boss Angel was confident that he would be alright.

Boss Angel gently lifted Jimi against a pillow and explained that he now had a second chance. As the crew arrived, they discovered Jimi Hendrix in his vomit-covered state. Boss Angel decided it would be best to have Jimi rushed to Saint Mary Abbott's Hospital, which was only two miles away from the Samarkand Hotel. The ambulance arrived at 11:45 AM, and Jimi was promptly taken to the resuscitation room. There, Dr. Martin Seifert conducted a thorough examination and determined that Jimi was completely revived.

Jimi spent the evening recuperating at the hospital and felt 100% the next morning. He then returned to the Samarkand Hotel and continued with his life and career. He was hailed as one of the greatest musicians to have ever lived. Boss Angel and Maggie were both content with Jimi's successful rescue and were eager to return to the United States to witness Achilles' reaction.

Mike Jeffery's only source of income was through Jimi Hendrix, which he would capitalize on if Jimi were to die or be murdered. What a horrible "experience" either way.

Chapter Eight
Teddy Pendergrass

Boss Angel, today's mission is to save Teddy Pendergrass, one of the greatest soul singers of all time.

Archangel, he is one of my all-time favorites, and it is heartbreaking to think that he became a paraplegic after a horrendous automobile accident. I gave everything I had to save Teddy, but even with all the godly powers we possess, we couldn't prevent the paralysis of his spine.

Achilles, I know you are all-knowing, and when it comes to saving lives, you have awareness of what will happen even before it occurs. Sadly,

Teddy's father, Jesse Pendergrass, was murdered by being stabbed to death by one of his own friends.

Teddy said he only seen his father twice in his whole life, buy that time Teddy fell in love with R&B music like James Brown and especially after he saw singer Jackie Wilson perform at the Uptown theater. How the ladies went crazy for him in his teenage years. Though Teddy did hang out with gangs, and he got in trouble spending time in the juvenile detention after a wrongful arrest for robbery.

For most part going to work with his mother who worked at a restaurant where a lot of famous stars would hang and most of the time just harmonize! That's where Teddy learned how to play drums, he didn't even use the drumsticks he was just use his fingers to play by ear! Now he started taking music seriously and he ended up meeting up with a number of different great vocalist recorded his first solo song title 'Angel with muddy feet' but the song went nowhere.

Teddy went back to playing drums. Then Teddy dropped out of high school and got an opportunity to be a drummer playing for a guy named Little Royal in different cities but see him and Little Royal had a falling out and they stopped working together. Then he started playing drums for other groups like the Cadillac.

At the same time Harold Melvin was part of a 50s doo-wop group called the blue notes! They had split up and Harold Melvin was looking for new members. After seeing Teddy and the Cadillac's perform one evening, Harold Melvin hired them on the spot! They began to perform in hotel lounges, clubs, just anywhere because they were all willing to perform in order to make money. Sometimes some of the members would be late for the shows and the club owners would dock their pay even though Teddy was the drummer of the group he also showed him that he could sing as well while playing drums.

That's when Harold Melvin realized that Teddy was gifted and made him the lead singer of the group. Once Teddy became lead singer, the group began to gain a fan base. People began to take notice especially of Teddy, with his smooth and soulful powerhouse of a voice.

Producers Gamble and Huff who had just started a record label called Philadelphia International Records, were watching the group perform, and liked what they heard! Gamble and Huff began working with the group and told his mother that Teddy's voice is the reason they want to work with Harold.

Once the contracts came around Harold Melvin took control and named the group Harold Melvin and the Blue notes! This way the money would come to Harold first, and everybody would think he was doing all the lead singing instead of Teddy. After signing the contract with Philadelphia International Records, Gamble and Huff, Harold Melvin and the Blue Notes released their first single called 'I miss you' which was originally written for

The Dells but they passed on it. Gamble and Huff decided to let Teddy sing that song, his voice reminded him of Marvin juniors. Though that song 'I miss you' made some noise in the industry, the second single title 'If you don't know me by now' became their first number one hit topping the US R&B charts and reaching number three on the US billboard Hot 100 and selling over 1,000,000 copies. That song was originally written for Patti LaBelle and the group 'LaBelle', but they never recorded it because they were too busy at the time.

Harold Melvin and the Blue Notes continued on to drop 'The love I lost' that went to number one, 'Wake up everybody' that went number one, 'Hope that we can be together soon' which featured female singer Sharon Page which went to number one and other songs and as the group continued to be successful.

Teddy got tired of fans calling him Harold Melvin. To make matters worse, Harold Melvin was in control of the group's money and was jealous of how the fans especially the ladies would go crazy over Teddy. Eventually Teddy just got fed up just made the decision to do his own thing.

Teddy decided to go with Huff and Gamble. The rest of the Blue Notes tried to convince Teddy to stay because they had already built a fan base, but Teddy was ready to move on and his new manager and girlfriend Tazi Lane was behind him 100%.

Now a solo artist with his own record deal with Gamble and Huff made Harold Melvin very angry. He was putting threats out on the Philly streets and actual contract hits on Teddy.

His new manager Tazi was very well known in Philly, because she was once married to Philadelphia running back Izzy lane. She was a model, she owned a beauty salon and was good friends with singers Deon Ward and Nancy Wilson.

After dating for two months, Teddy and Tazi broke up, but she remained his manager for Teddy Bear Productions. Months before releasing his debut album, Tazi Lane was shot to death! No one was ever convicted, and the case remains unsolved.

Rumors spread that Teddy had something to do with it, but he denied it. After her death in 1977, he released his self-titled album with the hits 'I don't love you anymore' and 'the whole town's laughing at me'. The album was certified platinum. His second album though, 'Life is a song worth singing' is the album that made Teddy the sex symbol for the ladies. Hits like 'close the door' spent two weeks at number one on the R&B chart and was certified gold. Other hits off that album include 'get up get down get funky get loose', 'it don't hurt now' and 'when Somebody Loves You back', pushing that album to double platinum.

Achilles, this was the string of hits that are unforgettable. I'm very surprised that he's one of your favorites you know with your Andy Williams and stuff like that.

Boss Angel don't let my looks fool you they've been around a very long time and sometimes people need a boost, and I gave all I could to Teddy but now it's time for you to step forward and bring him back.

Ok I'm ready just finish off his bio Achilles, so there can be no doubt.

Ok the hits kept rolling. 'Come go with me' 'Turn off the lights' Love 'TKO' Teddy was selling out plenty of arenas worldwide, calling him the black Elvis and also the Teddy bear! One tour he called for a woman only concert. Women of all races and audience members were given chocolate Teddy bear shaped lollipops! I mean they were throwing money on a stage going crazy for Teddy.

Man, during that time he had a lot of power in Philadelphia and a lot of people were jealous of him. When he went to the American Music Awards for favorite soul R&B male artist in 1979, Teddy got himself a Rolls Royce which was fine because it matched his 34-room mansion on 14 acres of land. Teddy even had his own jeans, they were called Teddy jeans.

Even Marvin Gaye appeared to be overly jealous of Teddy with his wife Jan, but nothing ever happened in a serious manner. There was mechanical proof the brake lines were cut on his vehicle and also on his sports car, but they could never actually prove who did it.

Marvin's irritation with Teddy became worse when Teddy grew a beard similar to Marvin's. Marvin continued to accuse Teddy and his wife Jan of having a relationship.

Boss Angel I think it is time for me to exit, I'm hearing much too many things, So I'm going to let you take over from here.

Ok Achilles I got this one. I'm going to interfere with the car accident, but I haven't quite figured it out yet, I'll contact you when this is over, see you back at the Biltmore.

Achilles evaporates, and puff like that, he's gone!

Boss Angel already knew about the affairs with other woman but didn't realize there were so many Including Marvin Gaye's wife Jan.

Rick James said he tried to give Teddy advice about the music business and told him to stop messing with other men's wives and girlfriends, but Teddy wouldn't listen to anyone. He also had problems with The Isley Brothers, Bobby Womack, among others. It seemed like everybody wanted a piece of Teddy.

It is now the night of Teddy's famous accident and Boss Angel is following behind Tanika Watson and Teddy Pendergrass. Boss Angel is trying to figure out how to intercept Teddy's Rolls Royce from hitting the two trees that he is destined for. Boss Angel stayed right behind them as they drove on the Expressway. As they got closer to the landmark of prior accident he was going to try to get in front of them and just slow them down a little at a time until the car comes to a stop, but Teddy made a wild swing around Boss Angels vehicle and picked up speed.

Boss Angel III

March 18th, 1982, Teddy after leaving the club with Tanika Watson, who was a transgender nightclub performer and prostitute whose real name was John Watson, was driving his Rolls Royce fast to get way. His brakes gave out and he lost control of the car, crashed into a guardrail hitting two trees.

Boss Angel couldn't believe that the same thing happened prior to this incident. He felt more of the blame and couldn't do anything about it. Teddy and Tanika were pinned in their car, and Boss Angel was unable to open the car doors to rescue Teddy and Tanika! It was almost an hour before help could arrive! Tanika somehow survived that crash with just minor injuries. Teddy was thrown into the back seat leaving him with a spinal cord injury that left him paralyzed from the chest down, leaving him a quadriplegic!

After the accident Teddy's sexuality would be called into question, and rumors began to fly that he was gay! Teddy never addressed the allegations. After spending six months in the hospital the doctors told him he probably only had seven years to live.

Once Teddy got home he was suicidal and trying to convince his girlfriend Karen to help him end this life by giving him an overdose of sleeping pills because he couldn't do it himself, he was paralyzed.

When the boss Angel returned to the Biltmore awaiting Achilles presence, he didn't know what he was going say other than the fact that he knew already Achilles knows everything that happens.

In walks Achilles to the Biltmore lounge area and says fear not Boss Angel for we have all made mistakes in the past and you wouldn't be working for me now if mistakes weren't made by my crew of angels. Even I have made a few!

Boss Angel tells Achilles you just don't understand, Teddy was my favorite singer, even over Frank Sinatra and Tony Bennett. Isn't there something we can do to bring him back to normal health?

No unfortunately we had a second chance for Teddy, it didn't happen. All we can do for him now is to make him want to sing again which will make him happy again and to make his family happy seeing him sing and seeing his joy with no more pain. It's out of our hands to bring him back. I'm sorry Boss Angel.

He has Karen who really loves Teddy though she used to be one of his dancers and she was there right by his side when he suffered severe depression and insomnia for years. It was her that made Teddy realized that his family and friends and the fans were supporting him. This motivated him to work and regain his strength and singing ability.

Teddy did marry Karen years later around 1987 and seemed ready to record but Teddy was having trouble getting a record deal because of his injury.

Asylum Records gave him a shot, though I believe it was Achilles who put in the extra hand.

Teddy recorded the album titled 'love language'. On that album was a duet 'Hold Me' with a then unknown 21-year-old singer named Whitney Houston. This become her first chart hit. She lost the Grammy for best new artist in 1985 because they didn't consider her new artist. She was part of the duet with Teddy.

In 1985 in front of almost 100,000 people and two billion viewers and 150 countries Teddy made a surprise appearance at the Live Aid concert in Philadelphia, his first public showing since the accident. In 1986 Teddy Put on an explosive show for the crowd which brought him back to life and gave him the confidence he was lacking since the accident.

Teddy Went on to make a half dozen albums and the boss Angel remembered seeing him in the wheelchair on stage at the casino in Connecticut.

I loved him then and I love him now.

Chapter Nine
Nicole Brown Simpson

Boss Angel sits at the bar inside the Biltmore lounge, eagerly awaiting the arrival of one of the two angels who will assign him his next mission. He calmly sips on Johnny Walker Blue, knowing that this will be his last drink of the night. However, before he gets the chance to finish it, his close friend JB walks in. Over the course of multiple missions, they have developed a strong bond.

"Hey, handsome, how have the missions been treating you?" JB asks.

Boss Angel sighs and replies, "JB, it seems like the more I do, the more difficult they become."

JB's tone turns serious as he says, "Well, unfortunately, I have something for you that I don't think you're going to like. Before I tell you, I think you should have another drink to brace yourself for this horrific next mission."

Boss Angel, already feeling the weight of the upcoming task, waves off JB's suggestion. "Forget the drink, JB. I've had enough already. Just tell me what it is."

OK just the name is going to shock you but here goes. Nicole Brown Simpson! "JB, you have got to be kidding me!" Boss Angel exclaims.

JB responds firmly, "Not only am I not kidding you, but Achilles is very serious about this tragic double death and the possibility of saving them."

Boss Angel's expression turns somber as he states, "I remember everything about that, JB. I was actually in Brentwood, CA during the incident. I stood outside OJ's house in the days that followed when he was arrested by the LAPD. Though they released him, the infamous white Bronco chase ensued. The unmistakable guilt was evident to everyone watching on TV until the chase finally concluded at his home."

JB is talking. "Alright, Boss Angel, I insist you have one more drink because I'm going to begin telling you the story in its entirety, and I believe you'll need a little more intoxication than what you have now." Boss Angel signals to the bartender, "I'll have another," while JB says, "Make that two." Both Boss Angel and JB drink simultaneously, taking a moment to savor their drinks before continuing. "Ahh, okay, I'm ready. Here goes."

"She was very spiritual and always had a smile on her face. For seven years, she was married to football hero OJ Simpson. OJ truly worshipped her, I mean really did. But behind that facade of a trophy wife, there was an ugly secret. I can't believe anyone would associate with a man like that. It's just terrible, and soon the dream will be shattered, leading to the bizarre freeway chase that will thrust

OJ Simpson into a media frenzy inside the courtroom."

This is the last 24 hours in the life of Nicole Brown Simpson. On June 11th, 1994, it's 10:40 PM, and Nicole Brown Simpson is soundly sleeping at her home located at 875 S Bundy Drive. For the past year, she has been residing in this affluent Brentwood neighborhood with her children, Sydney and Justin.

It has been two years since her divorce from OJ Simpson, and in just 24 hours, she will tragically lose her life unless someone like your Boss Angel can save her. The next morning, at 6:30 AM, Nicole Brown Simpson is already awake. As a fitness enthusiast, the 35-year-old starts her day with an early morning run. This is a common ritual in California, where looking good and staying fit is a priority. Nicole was dedicated to her fitness routine, often running about 9 miles a day. I'm amazed at her commitment and impressive physical shape.

Meanwhile, less than 10 miles away at the Riviera Country Club, Nicole's famous ex-husband, OJ Simpson, the retired football star and media celebrity, is also engaged in his early morning exercise. In his case, it involves teeing off with his Hollywood friends. Golf has become his primary sporting passion, and tonight he is scheduled to fly to Chicago to host a celebrity golf tournament for

Hertz Rent-A-Car, the company that contributes to his multi-millionaire status.

After seven years of marriage, Nicole Brown Simpson was adjusting to the single life. One person who knew her well during this time was her neighbor, Ron Hardy. They were introduced through mutual friends and lived about 200 yards apart. Ron spent a significant amount of time with Nicole and her children. They shared many mutual friends and often engaged in social activities together. During this phase of her life, Nicole had embraced her independence.

At this point, many men in her life were simply friends. She was starting to discover her own identity and wanted to enjoy life. Nicole found joy in spending time with her kids, bonding with her sisters, and socializing with friends.

She first met OJ Simpson back in 1977 while working at an upscale Hollywood club. One night, the man who would become her husband walked into the establishment, and their meeting was filled with undeniable chemistry. It was a love at first sight moment for both of them. Despite OJ Simpson's widespread fame, the young and naive Nicole had limited knowledge of football and only a vague idea of his true identity. To the majority of America, the man known as The Juice was both a sports legend and a Hollywood star. OJ persisted in visiting the restaurant frequently, determined to win over the beautiful Nicole. Seeking guidance, Nicole turned to David Laban, an old friend with whom she was sharing an apartment at the time. As soon as David learned that OJ Simpson had asked Nicole out, he provided her with all the information he knew about OJ. He was visibly impressed by the fact that a renowned running back and exceptional football player was interested in his friend.

Nicole was clearly outmatched as he was 30 and she was 18. He was a star and she worked in a restaurant. He was a multimillionaire she was broke. OJ's persistence paid off. JB, Nicole began to realize just who OJ Simpson was and his popularity, then she caved in!

OJ would pick her up in his black Rolls Royce, and his license plate said 'Juice.' Her friend David became concerned when one-night Nicole returned with ripped pants. She said he was just a little forceful. David was quite upset and wanted to talk to OJ, but Nicole brushed it off. Clearly from the start, it was no fairy tale.

At the time, OJ was married with two children. His wife Marguerite was pregnant with a third, but that didn't stop Nicole or OJ's jealous request that she immediately vacate her male roommate's apartment. He told her he didn't want her living with anybody, even though it was a completely platonic friendship. He got her an apartment of her own.

"Boss Angel replies, 'Isn't that spectacular that you can live with your wife having birthed two children, with one on the way, but expected Nicole to live solo?'"

OJ became more and more possessive of Nicole, and his jealousy grew. OJ Simpson allowed her to live the life of the rich and famous, like the rest of her neighbors in posh Brentwood, CA, with shopping sprees and Ferraris. This was a long way from her modest roots. She was the second of four daughters and was born in 1959 in Frankfurt, Germany, to Lou Brown, an American serviceman, and Judith, his German wife. In 1963, when Nicole was just 4 years old, the family moved to California, to the booming shores of Orange County. She was a little surf rat and grew up on the beach, always having her own little surfboard and surfing often with her sister, Denise, as they were the closest in age. The two sisters were the picture-perfect image of quintessential California girls. In high school, Nicole did some modeling, and she once told her class that when she grew up, she wanted to marry someone wealthy. Friend David Laban mentioned that after high school, she wanted to be a photographer.

After High School, Nicole had thoughts of becoming a photographer and a friend was teaching her how to take pictures. She contemplated photography school. She always had the best cameras and she always knew where the best light was but instead she followed her friend David to

Los Angeles in search of a job and moved in with him to split the expenses.

Her dazzling good looks trumped any other talent she may have had and led to a job as a hostess at The Daisy, an upscale Beverly Hills Club, where she greeted the stars and eventually met OJ Simpson. The Daisy was a private club and a hangout for movie stars. Everybody who was anybody would go there. When OJ first set eyes on the new hostess of The Daisy, he was a household name, but his football career was almost over, as was his marriage to Marguerite. After a three-year affair with Nicole, he finally divorced his first wife in February 1985 and then married the homecoming princess, Nicole Brown, in a ceremony at his

Rockingham mansion. It was a fabulous night and a great party. They set up their house at the Rockingham mansion, and by 1988 they had two children, a girl named Sydney and a boy named Justin. They were the epitome of wedded bliss. OJ, the football legend, loved to be seen with sexy Nicole on his arm. She enjoyed going to charity functions and meeting a lot of stars and wealthy people. While Nicole was not a celebrity wife who wanted to be in the limelight, she loved the Hollywood glam scene. She had a casual style and could be seen any day in flip flops and shorts.

    Jesus, JB, do I have to go through this entire double homicide? Yes, you do. It's a little added seasoning for you to swallow. Now come on, pay attention!

In 1988, she had a $5,000,000 mansion surrounded by the cream of Hollywood, a condo in New York, and a $2,000,000 seafront house in Laguna Beach, complete with his and her Ferraris. She was known to drive her Ferrari down to the beach. There were endless vacations, often with her sisters in tow. She would take her sisters skiing and to New York. They seemed very happy during this time. Just like all victims, it wasn't all bad.

Unfortunately, OJ would let his jealousy get the best of him, and the football legend frequently flew into rages. However, Nicole was feisty and stood her ground. She could just push his buttons, and he could go off. OJ was a very controlling person, and it was always about him.

Not knowing what to do, Nicole turned to therapist Dr. Susan. She was in disbelief that this was actually domestic violence, even though it started long before they were married.

JB, what I don't understand is if the domestic violence carried on like they say it did, then why didn't the poor girl just leave? Boss Angel, here's the reason: she lived in the neighborhood where she could just walk down the street to 360 north Rockingham aver That was OJ's mansion. Where the children had lived not far from Nicole condo. Apparently, she didn't believe that he would harm her, not including the punches and kicks he administered to her.

It is well-documented that domestic violence is common among professional athletes, especially football players, due to their exposure to a violent world. There is also a warped sense of self where they believe they are invincible and can act with impunity.

It was known that OJ had a collection of knives. Friends began to fear that he would use a knife on his wife. OJ even threatened to slice her up, and the ongoing fights between them escalated. Nicole became afraid and eventually called the police. However, little did she know that the police would soon be called to investigate her own brutal double murder.

Boss Angel puts together, what appears to be the only viable plan. He will go to Nicole's condo 10 minutes before the recorded history of these murders.

On June 12th, 1994, at 11:30 am, Nicole Brown Simpson had spent the morning shopping for her kids. She had bought a dozen yellow roses for her daughter Sydney, who would be performing at a recital that night. Little did she know it would be the last time she would see her eight-year-old daughter dance. In just 11 hours, Nicole Brown Simpson would be assaulted.

OJ Simpson is playing a leisurely game of gin rummy at his country club with his Hollywood friends. Later, Simpson would say that he was killing time before attending Sydney's dance rehearsal and then catching a flight to Chicago. It's a long way from San Francisco's housing projects where Simpson was born in 1947, named Orenthal James Simpson. He hated his name even as a child and was known as OJ or inevitably, the juice. The name stuck with him throughout his football years. His family was poor, and due to a lack of vitamins in his diet, young OJ suffered from rickets, which ironically forced the future All-Star running back to wear a corrective leg brace during his childhood years. Being a football player, I believe there was still some violence in him.

After the dance recital, OJ left, but not without trying to talk to Nicole, who did not want to hear anything from him! She just did not wanna speak to him at all or talk to him whatsoever. It was getting close to the time of the massacre! It appears OJ went home to get dressed for his Chicago trip, even though there were a few hours remaining before he took off. Boss Angel went to his hotel room to change into an all-black outfit. It was getting closer to the time, less than 20 minutes to be exact. Boss Angel got his rental car and drove to Nicole's condo. He parked behind Nicole's condo. Both Angel parked right next to Nicole's canary yellow Ferrari. Suddenly, he heard some screaming which sounded like OJ in front. It would have been nice to have had JB along for the trip, but he said that one must stay clear and those are Achilles' orders!

Boss Angel opens the back gate leading down the walkway on the side of the condo to the front yard of Nicole's unit. As Boss Angel approaches the front, he hears the arguing escalating into violent screams. To his surprise, he sees a figure that appears to be OJ wearing a wool hat on his head and holding a knife in his hand, even wearing a pair of black leather gloves! It was 82 degrees outside, so wearing gloves seems very peculiar. This feels like a nightmare. As OJ notices Boss Angel, he takes a moment to assess the situation and sees Ron Goldman lying motionless to his left. Further down the walkway, Nicole is lying in a pool of blood. Boss Angel is beside himself, unable to comprehend the horrific scene unfolding before his eyes. The argument that he had heard when he got out of the car turned out to be Nicole and Ron being stabbed to death.

Boss Angel instantly teleports himself back to the Biltmore. He needs to explain the situation to Achilles, but to his surprise, JB is already at the bar enjoying a drink. Boss Angel recounts the whole incident, mentioning that he was slightly delayed while OJ arrived early. He then asks JB if he thinks Achilles would be willing to give him another chance.

"JB, come on, you know there only one chance," JB responds. "Let's face it, you already know there's no room for an extra save. This was my mistake, and I understand that I only have one shot."

"I'm going to convince Achilles to give me another opportunity!" Boss Angel declares. "I won't need another soul, and if Achilles grants me that chance, I won't fail this time!"

"Good luck, my friend," JB replies. "Achilles just stepped out of the elevator. Achilles approaches Boss Angel, Achilles knows exactly what happened and he's very upset about it. So, upset in fact Boss Angel can see it on his face! He's going to make an attempt because after all OJ arrived 10 minutes earlier, and I was right on time. Achilles, you know the mission failed, and Ron Goldman and Nicole Brown Simpson remain deceased! Achilles tells Boss Angel, "I heard through the grapevine you're seeking another attempted save with Ron Goldman and Nicole Brown Simpson! You can just forget about it, Boss Angel. Even I can't give another soul or save. I'm not telling you what you can and can't do; I'll let you figure that out. But here is your next save. Prepare yourself."

Chapter Ten
Michael Jackson

Boss Angel, for the very first time, has been asked by Achilles the Archangel to go and have drinks while waiting for his next assignment at "Capriccios Restaurant" This place is very familiar to Boss Angel because he held his wedding reception there in '92 with his first wife. It's peculiar that he is being summoned by Achilles to a different location to receive his mission. As Boss Angel watches Achilles comes down the stairs with Maggie following him. He can sense that something special is about to happen in this mission. They both approach Boss Angel's table and sit down. Achilles tells Boss Angel that this mission is separate from all the previous successful ones he has completed. Maggie wearing a white sparkle gloves on both hands, intervenes and says that this may be the most important save that you, Boss Angel have ever done. Boss Angel asks why have they chose Capriccios, considering that you both know I was married there. Achilles explains that Capriccios is well-known for its first-class style, and great cuisine. Your mission today is to make this save. And comes straight from the top. Confused Boss Angel asks what Achilles means by the "top" and expresses his belief that Achilles is the highest authority around. Achilles responds by saying, "No, I'm afraid not. I just take orders, but typically I do a lot of repair work as an Archangel. Boss Angel, eager to know more, asks

Achilles to reveal the details, as the tension is increasing. Achilles agrees and unveils that Boss Angel's next mission is to save the King of Pop, the King of Rock, the King of Soul, Michael Jackson!

Really, it sounds complicated, but I'm up for the challenge. Maggie will provide you with all the information that will surprise and mesmerize you. It is important for us Angel that you pay attention to every word she says. Maggie assures Boss Angel, "We can do this, and Achilles will be there to support us if we need help." Instead of referring to him as the King of Pop, we prefer to call him Michael and tell you about his life. Michael was born on August 29th, 1958, in a two-bedroom house on Jackson Street in the small town of Gary,

Indiana. He was the eighth of ten children in a working-class African American Jackson family. Gary is located 25 miles from downtown Chicago, where Joseph Walter Joe Jackson settled when he was 18. It was there that he met his future wife, Catherine Esther Jackson. According to family lore, Joe's great-grandfather, Jack Gale, was a U.S. Army scout and Native American medicine man. After getting married, Joe and Catherine moved into a two-bedroom house on the corner of Jackson Street and 23rd Avenue.

Joe, an aspiring boxer and musician, played guitar in a local rhythm and blues band called the Falcons. However, he realized that supporting his family should be his priority. So, he took a job as a welder and crane operator at US Steel. At the same time, he pursued his passion for music, being a singer and a pianist with aspirations of becoming a country western performer. Meanwhile, Joe's wife, while working part-time at Sears, encouraged their children's musical talent. They had three sisters named, Rebbie, LaToya and Janet. and five brothers named Jackie, Tito, Jermaine, Marlon, and Randy. Unfortunately, their brother Brandon died shortly after birth. Michael had been involved with music since childhood, as their family was always singing together. They would even clear out the furniture from the living room and dance while washing dishes or playing music. One day, Michael's brother Tito broke their father's rule by touching his guitar and accidentally breaking a string. Tito hid this secret for a long time, fearing punishment. However, when their father eventually found out, he demanded that Tito show him what he could do.

He came up with the idea of creating a family group in 1964, along with the kids. Michael, at the age of 6, joined his brothers as a backing musician, playing congas and tambourine. The group, formed by their father, already included Jackie, Tito, Jermaine, and Marlon. However, Michael's childhood was different from that of other children. Jermaine recalled how Michael would look out the window at the streets decorated for Christmas, observing all the festivities from inside their house with no tree, lights, or decorations. Their tiny house was the only one without any Christmas decorations, making them feel like the only ones in Gary, Indiana without them. Their mother assured them that other homes and other Jehovah's Witnesses celebrated Christmas differently, but it did little to clear their confusion. They could see something that made them feel good, yet they were told it wasn't good for them. Their father was strict and sometimes cruel towards the boys, especially Michael. Joe would physically and emotionally abuse him during rehearsals. Joe often sat in a chair with a belt in his hand, ready to punish Michael and his siblings when they made mistakes. While Joe later claimed that he did not beat them but rather regularly spanked them, Catherine, Michael's mother, believed that spanking, which eventually

Maggie Getting hit with the belt was very common back in the 50s and 60s which came to be considered abuse, was the most common way to discipline children during Michael's upbringing. Jackie, Tito, Jermaine, and Marlon denied that their father abused them, referring to the spankings as disciplinary measures. Nevertheless, Michael, reminiscing about his youth, described it as lonely and isolated. Boss Angel says it seem It was always an issue for Michael, Maggie nods with Knowledge of the family.

Michael once confided in Oprah Winfrey, revealing that he had been so afraid of his father that it made him physically ill. In 2003, Michael recounted, "I just remember hearing my mother say,

'Stop it.'" Many years later, at the Grammy ceremony, the world-famous Michael Jackson would admit that his childhood had been taken away from him. There were no traditional celebrations like Christmas or birthdays. His upbringing was far from ordinary, lacking the typical joys of childhood. Instead, his early years were filled with hard work, struggle, and pain, eventually leading to immense material and professional success. Michael acknowledged that he couldn't recreate that part of his life, but he wouldn't change a thing. Over time, he began to share lead vocals with his brother Jermaine. The group's name was changed to the Jackson 5 in 1965. In that same year, the group achieved early success by winning a talent show and performing the song "My Girl" by The Temptations with Michael famously performing barefoot. This marked the beginning of the future star's career, and Joe, the father, quickly transitioned to become Joe, the manager.

He made the children call him Joseph, a strict taskmaster. Joe would put his sons through long and grueling rehearsals, determined to make their songs and performances perfect. It was this oppressive childhood experience that Michael would come to despise for the rest of his life. "You call me Joseph, Michael," he would say. Sister Janet recalled that after she once referred to him as "dad," he sternly corrected her, stating, "I'm Joseph to you."

The Jackson 5, based in the Midwest from 1966 to 1968, regularly performed in local auditoriums, school dances, and black clubs known as the chitlin circuit. They had the opportunity to be the opening act for famous groups such as Sam and Dave, the O'jays, Gladys Knight, and Etta James. Performing in nightclubs became a regular part of the Jackson Five's upbringing. Unfortunately, when Michael was only 7 or 8 years old, he was exposed to the adult nature of these venues. He witnessed striptease girls removing all their clothes, fights breaking out, and people vomiting on each other. Despite these experiences, the band continued to pursue their dreams and attended weekly amateur night concerts at the Apollo Theater in Harlem during their East Coast tour in August 1967.

Recognizing their potential, Joe made the decision to turn the Jackson 5 professional.

After a couple of years, he would sign a contract with the label with artists like Stevie Wonder, The Supremes, and Smokey Robinson. The Jackson 5 recorded several songs for Gary Stilltown Records label. They released their first single "Big Boy" in 1968. Bobby Taylor, of Bobby Taylor and the Vancouvers, brought the Jackson 5 to Motown. Wait a minute Maggie, I remember Diana Ross as being the one who introduced the Jackson 5. Nope Not true says Achilles. They performed for Taylor at Chicago's Regal Theatre. Later that year, Taylor produced some of their early recordings, including a version of "Who's Loving You." The Jackson family moved to Los Angeles after starting the contract with Motown the following year. Motown executives decided that Diana Ross should introduce the Jackson 5 to the public by shipping a fresh Motown product from her production line. The Jackson Five first appeared on television in 1969 at the Miss Black America contest, performing a cover of "It's Your Thing." Rolling Stone would later single out a young Michael as a prodigy with overwhelming musical gifts, who quickly emerged as the main draw and lead singer of "I Want You Back." It became the first Jackson Five song to hit #1 on the US Billboard Hot 100. The following January, the band's first album, "Diana Ross Presents The Jackson Five," hit the charts in

December of 1969 with the songs "ABC," "The Love You Save," and "I'll Be There." With a busy touring and recording schedule under the supervision of Barry Gordy and his Motown staff, the group became so popular that they even had a cartoon show that ran from 1971 to 1972.

At the same time, Michael began his solo musical career when he was 13. When he was 14, he released the album "Ben," which featured the eponymous ballad, Jackson's first solo number one single. Jackson transitioned from a child performer to a teen idol between 1972 and 1975. With the Jackson 5 in overtime, they were described as a cutting-edge example of black crossover artists. The group sold over 100 million records worldwide. The performance of their top-five single "Dancing Machine" on the TV show Soul Train popularized the robot dance. Despite the group's great success, there were problems behind the scenes, with tensions mounting over the management of the children's careers. The Jacksons wanted more creative control over their material. The band officially ended their contract with Motown in 1976. However, with the label, to continue his solo career, the Jackson 5 signed a contract with Epic Records and changed their name to the Jacksons. Their younger brother Randy joined the group, and the Jacksons continued to tour worldwide and released six albums between 1976 and 1984. Michael, being the band's writer at the time, wrote songs such as

"Shake Your Body (Down to the Ground)." Quincy Jones was responsible for arranging the music, and their acquaintance was a key event for Michael. It was he who would later produce Michael's three solo albums. Michael's solo album "Off the Wall" was released in 1979 to overwhelmingly positive response. The album helped the Jacksons' band as well. "Triumph" was released a little later and sold over 1,000,000 copies.

The brothers put on a big tour supporting the record. At the same time, Michael continued to look for new ways of self-development. The release of "Off the Wall" became Michael's first big success as a solo artist. However, during a dance program, he fell and broke his nose. The rhinoplasty that followed led to breathing problems that would later affect his career. This was likely his first plastic surgery, where he consulted Steven Hoffman, who became Jackson's lead surgeon. Over time, the familiar appearance of the star began to change in numerous interviews. In a 2002 interview with ABC News, Michael denied having done anything other than his nose, stating, "I've had no plastic surgery on my face, just my nose. It helped me breathe better so I can hit higher notes." In 1980, Michael Jackson received three American Music Awards for his solo work. He also won a Grammy Award for Best Male R&B Vocal Performance for "Don't Stop 'Til You Get Enough" in 1979.

Jackson felt that "Off the Wall" should have a significant impact and was determined to exceed expectations with his next release. It was amazing how the underwhelming music in "Me" and "Forever, Michael" led the way to the phenomenal "Off the Wall." The infectious mix of pop and funk stormed into the dance world. The album included the Grammy award-winning single "Don't Stop 'Til You Get Enough," as well as hits like "Rock with You" and "She's Out of My Life." In that regard, since the early '80s, the artist has received the highest royalty rate in the music industry, earning 38% of wholesale album profits. But it wasn't yet the pinnacle of Michael's career. The album "Thriller" was released in 1982 and immediately became the best-selling album in history, with seven top-ten hits. It stayed on the charts for 80 weeks, 37 of which were in first place worldwide. Over 70 million copies have been sold worldwide. In addition to its unprecedented commercial success, "Thriller" received 12 nominations at the 26th Grammy Awards and won eight, setting a record. Jackson's success demonstrated the varied nature of his work and showcased his songwriting talents. He received a Grammy Award for Best Rhythm and Blues Song for "Billie Jean" and was honored for the singles "Thriller" as Best Male Pop Vocal Performance and "Beat It" as Best Male Rock Vocal Performance.

Michael shared the Album of the Year award with co-producer Quincy Jones. There was

Jackson's joint track with Paul McCartney, "The Girl Is Mine," which almost reached the top of the pop charts. Here's how Paul McCartney recalled the beginning of the collaboration: "Michael originally rang me and said, 'You wanna make some hits?' I replied, 'Really? Yeah, sure I do.' So, he came over, and we agreed to meet here. Michael originally fancied writing some stuff for me, and I thought it was a good idea. So, he came over here to England, and we just hung out for a little while and got to know each other a bit. We ended up writing two songs."

The lead and self-titled single from the album "Thriller" received an elaborate music video. John Landis directed the horror-tinged video, which featured complex dance scenes, special effects, and a voiceover by actor Vincent Price. The clip was a huge success, further increasing the sales of an already highly popular record. In the video, Jackson underwent a metamorphosis, transforming from a human to a werewolf, then back to a human and finally into a zombie before returning to his human form. It was as if he was using the story to foreshadow the dramatic changes that would occur in his real life.

Meanwhile, in 1983, Michael went on his last tour with his brothers, supporting their album "Victory." One of the biggest hits on the record was Jackson's duet with Mick Jagger on "State of Shock." Jagger recalled, "We practiced scales for two hours, and then we recorded the vocals in no time. When he sent me the finished track later, I was kind of disappointed in the production and mix, but I think he's a really good singer." Mick replaced another legend in that song, as Michael Jackson had initially been recording with someone else.

The song recorded in the studio was with Queen singer Freddie Mercury for their joint album from 1981 to 1983, according to Queen's manager Jim Beach. The musicians' friendship was spoiled when Michael brought a llama to the studio. He was also frustrated with Mercury's drug use. Their joint compositions were only released in 2014 after the death of both musicians.

After the release of Victory, Michael and his brothers appeared on Motown 25 (yesterday today forever) in the NBC television special. Jackson performed his number one hit, "Billie Jean," and introduced the world to his soon-to-be-famous moonwalk dance move. Contrary to popular belief, Michael did not invent the moonwalk. Bill Bailey and Jeffrey Daniel had been using the dance move long before, and it was Daniel who Michael copied and asked to teach him. "I've been practicing the moonwalk for some time, and it dawned on me in our kitchen that I could finally do the moonwalk in public on Motown 25." The moonwalk was already prevalent on the streets, originating as a breakdance step created by black kids on the street corners in the ghetto. "So, I said, this is my chance to do it." Michael kept it in his head like an ace in the hole, carefully choosing the moment to show it to the public. He became the popularizer of the moonwalk and often used it, later directing the dance for the music video of another hit from the album, "Beat It." By the way, Jackson is the only musician in the American Dancers Hall of Fame, and his unique choreographic style remains famous to this day.

"I always knew how to dance," he said more than once. The choreography was already present in Jackson's earliest performances. As part of the Jackson Five, he recalled being a child alone behind the scenes, watching all of the headliners and learning from them as much as possible. He observed their feet, their hand movements, and how they held the microphone, trying to understand why they never missed a step or a moment, how they turned, twisted, and expressed their emotions through their movements. This was his education and his recreation.

His performance of "Billie Jean" earned him his first Emmy Award nomination. His performance was compared to those of Elvis Presley and The Beatles on the Ed Sullivan show.

The success has turned Jackson into a dominant force in global pop culture and cemented his status as the King of Pop! Jackson had the highest royalty rate in the music industry at the time, around $2.00 for each album sold, equivalent to $5 in 2022. He was making record profits.

Additionally, dolls were created based on Michael's appearance, priced at $12.00 each. There was also a documentary about the making of Michael Jackson's Thriller, which won the Grammy Award for Best Music Video in the same year! The New York Times wrote, "In the world of pop music, there is Michael Jackson, and then there is everyone else."

Jackson's influence at that point was as a star of records, radio, rock, and video. He was an A1 rescue team for the music business - a songwriter who set the beat for a decade, a dancer with the fanciest feet on the street, and a singer who transcended boundaries of taste, style, and color. On May 14th, 1984, President Ronald Reagan presented Michael Jackson with an award for his charity work supporting drug and alcohol abusers. This recognition was in appreciation of his support for the ad councils and the National Highway Traffic Safety administration's drunk driving prevention campaign. Michael allowed the use of "Beat It" in their social ads.

Jackson did not miss the opportunity to act in films and commercials. In November of 1983, he and his brothers partnered with PepsiCo in a $5,000,000 advertising deal, which marked a record-breaking celebrity endorsement. Today, this amount would be approximately $13.5 million. They needed that money to cover the cost of a massive tour campaign in the US from 1983 to 1984, focused on the new generation. This campaign included tour sponsorships, public relations events, and more. Jackson helped create the ad and suggested that his song, "Billie Jean," be used as the jingle with a slight change in the lyrics. On January 27th, 1984, when Michael and other members of the Jacksons filmed a Pepsi commercial, he, who didn't drink Pepsi, was supposed to star in two commercials.

He made sure that his face appeared on them as little as possible so as not to draw attention to himself. There was an embarrassing incident on the set of one of the videos during a concert in front of fans when pyrotechnics accidentally set Michael's hair on fire, causing second-degree burns to his scalp. Jackson underwent treatment to hide his scars and also had another rhinoplasty.

Pepsi settled the incident out of court, and Michael donated $1.5 million of his compensation to Brockman Medical Center. Later, he signed a new $10 million contract with Pepsi! He also worked with LA Gear, Suzuki, and Sony.

Michael was altruistic and often donated large sums to charity from that moment on. For example, during the same tour, the Jacksons came up with an unethical scheme to receive additional income from ticket sales. It involved assuming a money transfer of $120.00 instead of $30 to participate in a lottery with a possibility of getting 4 tickets in return. The funds for the losers would take 6 to 8 weeks to be returned, and the brothers expected to earn $10 to $12 million from the accrued interest. However, Michael was the only one who opposed such an idea. He believed that the $30 ticket price was already high compared to most touring performers, and the inclusion of 4 tickets made it even more unaffordable for many of his African American fans. Despite the high-ticket price, the singer still donated approximately $5,000,000.

Michael was disappointed when his idol James Brown turned down his invitation to join the band on stage at Madison Square Garden in New York City. Due to Brown's "I'm going outrage" over the ticket lottery, even before the tour was half completed, the brothers traveled to shows in different cars, traveled on different planes, stayed on different floors of their hotels, and refused to talk to each other on the way to shows.

From that point on, Michael was often represented by two lawyers - one for Germaine and another for Jackie, Tito, and Marlon. It was the worst experience Michael ever had with his brothers. Some were jealous, while others were in denial. The whole gamut of human emotions. During the final show of the Victory Tour at Dodger Stadium in Los Angeles, Jackson announced his split from the Jacksons!

The New York Times was absolutely right when they wrote, "In the world of pop music, there was Michael Jackson, and there is everyone else!" Michael's charitable work continued when he released "We Are the World" the following year. Co-written with Lionel Richie, the single raised funds for the poor people of the US and Africa. Stars such as Lionel Richie, Ray Charles, Bob Dylan, Willie Nelson, Bruce Springsteen, and Tina Turner also participated in the project. The track earned $63 million, equivalent to $158,000,000 in 2021, and became one of the best-selling singles of all time, selling 20 million copies. Additionally, the song won four Grammy Awards in 1985. Jackson donated $455,000 to the United Negro College Fund.

All profits from his single 'Man in the Mirror' went to charity. By that point, Michael's health continued to deteriorate, and Jackson's skin was medium brown. But from the mid-1980s, it gradually turned pale. The change received a lot of media coverage, including rumors that he bleached his skin. His dermatologist, Arnold Klein, said that in 1983, Jackson came to him for acne treatment. The doctor recognized lupus for the first time. They met, he did a biopsy, and diagnosed Michael with lupus erythematosus. At the same time, he observed and diagnosed "Oligo" in Jackson. It is a disease characterized by areas of the skin losing their pigment and sensitivity to sunlight. In an interview, Michael said that it began after the release of 'Thriller,' and at that time, he didn't know what it was initially. Jackson tried to cover his vitiligo patches with black makeup because he thought his appearance would harm his career. Then he wanted to hide uneven color spots using creams, which further lightened his skin, and he would appear very pale with makeup. Michael said that he didn't intentionally whiten his skin and couldn't control the vitiligo. The media claimed that Jackson intentionally wanted lighter skin and reduced his nose and lips, apparently trying to look for the last straw of changing the color. Michael's skin was the release of 'Black or White,' and it seemed to the public that the performer was teasing expanse skin color in the video. In an interview with Oprah Winfrey, Michael denied those claims, saying there is no such thing as skin whitening. "I've never seen it. I have a skin disorder that destroys the pigmentation of the skin. It's something that I cannot help, OK? But when people make up stories that I don't want to be who I am, it hurts me."

In his 1988 autobiography and 1993 interview, Michael claimed to have had two rhinoplasty operations and a cleft chin operation, but nothing more. He mentioned that his weight loss in the early 1980s was due to a diet to achieve a lean dancer's figure. It was reported that Michael often felt dizzy, and there were rumors that he suffered from anorexia nervosa. Periods of weight loss became a recurring problem later in his life. In 1986, tabloids reported that Jackson slept in a hypodermic oxygen chamber to slow aging and depicted him lying in a glass box. However, these claims were false. The tabloids reported that he spread the story himself. They also reported that Jackson injected himself with female hormones to keep his voice high and facial hair thin. Approved creams for the treatment of vitiligo were found in his home. These creams remove and lighten the remaining pigment. In a TV show, a client said that vitiligo became too severe and it was difficult to cover it with makeup. His skin had to be deep pigmented with creams. The condition remained stable, but Jackson had to repeat the treatment from time to time. It was difficult to darken depigmented skin, and the deep pigmentation caused permanent and extreme sensitivity to the sun. This put patients at risk of contracting melanoma, and they were advised to undergo annual cancer screening. Therefore, Jackson often hid his skin.

Though he would only be seen in sunlight with an umbrella, in long sleeves and trousers, and appeared in the sun during the 80s, he took good care of his chimpanzee, Bubbles. Michael Jackson kept Bubbles, a chimpanzee, as a pet. He bought Bubbles from a Texas Research Center and traveled with him, turning Bubbles into a media star as well. Michael took the chimpanzee on a tour of Japan, and the media portrayed him as an aspiring Disney cartoon character. In 1988, Michael decided to move to Neverland Ranch and took Bubbles along. Bubbles slept in his bed and used Michael's bathroom and shower. While at Neverland, Bubbles grew from a small chimp to a huge adult chimpanzee. Due to his size and aggressive behavior, Bubbles became unsuitable as a pet, like many captive chimpanzees, and was sent to an animal trainer in California.

At the same time, Jackson was working with George Lucas and Francis Ford Coppola on the $30 million seventeen-minute 3D film, "Captain EO." Lucas was the screenwriter and Coppola was the director. The film was completed in 1986 and aired with additional effects of laser sand smoke. It was showcased at Disneyland and Epcot, and later at Tokyo Disneyland and Euro Disneyland until the late 90s. However, Disney wanted to change Michael's voice because they thought it was too high, and they were afraid that people wouldn't take him seriously. The singer was unaware of the decision until he found out that Lucas had vetoed it in.

In 1987, Jackson separated from and left the Jehovah's Witnesses, perhaps because some witnesses opposed the "Thriller" video. Nevertheless, for a long time, Michael did not release any new material. Finally, after five years of waiting, he released a new album called "Bad." Many expected him to repeat the great success of the previous one, and they were right. The release served as a follow-up to "Thriller" and reached the top of the charts with a record-breaking five number one hits: "I Just Can't Stop Loving You," "Bad," "The Way You Make Me Feel," "Man in the Mirror," and "Dirty Diana." The album's title track was supported by a video directed by Martin Scorsese. Another popular track from the album, "Smooth Criminal," only reached 7th place on the charts but was beloved by fans and received an achievement at the American Music Awards.

Thanks to a record number of #1 singles and being the first album to top the charts in 25 countries, "Bad" became the best-selling album worldwide in 1987 and 1988. The Bad World Tour lasted almost a year and a half, with 14 sell-outs in Japan and setting a new attendance record of 570,000 people, nearly three times the previous record. Additionally, the tour collected 504,000 listeners across seven sold-out shows at Wembley Stadium, setting a new Guinness World Record.

In an interview with the album Michael resent his philosophy, if you want to make the world a better place take a look at yourself and then make a change. People don't look at themselves honestly and they don't look at themselves and point the finger, it's always the other guy's fault or somebody else should change themselves to look at yourself make better place and look at yourself!

He has come a long way and gone through many internal and external changes, always keeping an idea of making a positive impact. In an interview, when Michael was asked if he was happy when he looked in the mirror, he said that he's never totally satisfied. He always wished the world could be a better place, and he hoped to achieve that through his music by bringing happiness and joy to people. He believed that they needed some peace in their lives.

In 1988, Michael released his autobiography, "Moonwalk." The book sold over 200,000 copies and reached the top of the New York Times bestseller list. In it, Michael wrote about his childhood, the Jackson 5, and the abuse he suffered from his father. He also explained the changes in his appearance, including undergoing three plastic surgeries, experiencing puberty and weight loss, adopting a strict vegetarian diet, changing his hairstyle, and even having a life-changing experience while visiting Paris during a tour.

Michael was awarded the Romil Medal of the city of Paris by Mayor Jacques Chirac. In October, he released the film Moonwalker, which showcased live footage and short films featuring Jackson and Joe Pesci. The film became the best-selling videotape in the US and has been certified eight times platinum by the RIAA.

Michael Jackson purchased 2,700 acres or approximately 11 square kilometers of land near Santa Cruz, CA, in March of 1988. The land was covered with plane trees and live oaks, and it was located near the coast, providing cool breezes and moist soil. Vineyards surrounded the territory, and the property was situated on the edge of the Los Padres National Forest. Michael invested $17 million in the land, which would be equivalent to about $40 million today. He proceeded to build various attractions on the property, including a Ferris wheel, carousel, lake with a waterfall, railway, cinema for 50 spectators, basketball and tennis courts, and a zoo featuring elephants, giraffes, chimpanzees, crocodiles, snakes, and a bear.

Guests frequently visited the ranch, including many famous children. In 1995, Michael brought 46 children from around the world to the World Congress of Children. Initially called Sycamore Valley Ranch, he later renamed it Neverland, after the magical land where children never grow up in the book Peter Pan. During his time at the ranch, Michael fostered a carnival-like atmosphere and enjoyed spending time with the children. Perhaps he was trying to recapture the fun he missed during his own childhood.

When the architect received a call from Michael regarding the future Neverland, he initially disbelieved it and hung up. He was shocked when

Michael explained his construction plans and recalled that Michael was more like a little kid, wanting things immediately, rather than being demanding.

    He had crews working all hours of the day, and it was evident that Michael was excited. He pushed the architect and contractor, but it was a different kind of pressure, more of a fun pressure. Michael gave the contractor a clear mental image of his vision and allowed him the freedom to bring it to life. Meanwhile, he also performed at Sammy Davis Jr.'s 60th birthday celebration. Jackson earned a second Emmy nomination and became the best-selling artist of the 1980s.

They called him the King of Pop, and the nickname literally stuck to him. In 1989, when Elizabeth Taylor presented him with the Soul Train Heritage Award, she referred to him as the true King of Pop, Rock, and Soul! President George H.W. Bush designated him as the White House's artist of the decade. In March of 1991, Jackson extended his contract with Sony and released his eighth album, Dangerous, co-produced with Teddy Riley. It was symbolic that the album achieved eight times platinum status in the United States! The following year, it became the best-selling album worldwide.

While it didn't reach the same level of phenomenal success as his previous album, a couple of songs from Dangerous topped the charts worldwide. The song "Black or White" even stayed in first place for seven weeks. Worth mentioning is the music video for the song, directed by Landis and featuring a cameo appearance by child star Macaulay Culkin. The video's controversial ending, which depicted Michael's actions as potentially sexual gestures, surprised and shocked many viewers. It was only the beginning of a growing scandal.

While 1992 wasn't particularly productive for Michael in the musical realm, it was significant in terms of social impact. He launched the Heal the World Foundation, a charity aimed at helping underprivileged children enjoy theme park rides on ranches and providing millions of dollars worldwide to aid children affected by war, poverty, and disease.

In July, Michael published his second book, Dancing the Dream, which was a collection of poetry inspired by the death of his friend and HIV/AIDS spokesperson, Ryan White. Michael passionately urged the administration of Bill Clinton's inaugural gala to allocate more funds to charity, specifically for HIV/AIDS research. He emphasized the importance of supporting these causes. Michael remarked, "We're just creating a replica of nature, which is the sounds we hear outside!"

In the meantime, Jackson's music remained immensely popular, and he performed at numerous prominent events. The following year, he even took part in the Super Bowl 27 halftime show, which garnered more viewers than the game itself! In January, Michael Jackson received three American Music Awards: Favorite Pop/Rock Album, Favorite Soul/R&B Single, and he became the first artist to win the International Artist Award of Excellence in February.

He won the Living Legend Award at the 35th Annual Grammy Awards and attended the award show with Brooke Shields. Michael's relationships were complicated. He dated Oscar winner Tatum O'Neill, and they became friends when he was 12 and she was 17. However, by 1982, their relationship had cooled. Later, Michael met Brooke Shields and even considered marrying her, but Shields was not enthusiastic about the idea. She once told Michael, "You have me for the rest of your life, you don't need to marry me!" There were also reports of a brief relationship between Michael and Madonna, although according to Madonna, it didn't go beyond three dates and a kiss on the tongue. Rumors circulated that he had a short relationship with Shana Mangal and Whitney Houston, whom he allegedly wanted to marry quickly in August of 1993.

    Michael's career took a dramatic turn that would forever alter it when 13-year-old Jordan Chandler and his father, Evan Chandler, accused the singer of child sexual abuse. These initial allegations set the stage for a disturbing chain of events. Jordan claimed that he and Michael Jackson engaged in kissing and oral sex. Initially, the boy's mother stated to the police that she didn't believe Jackson had molested her son, but her stance later changed. Even Michael's older sister, La Toya, accused him of pedophilia. However, she later revealed that her ex-husband coerced her into making these accusations.

A few days following the allegations, the police conducted a search of Michael's home and discovered two legally obtained large format art books featuring boys playing, running, and swimming in various stages of undress. Michael denied having any knowledge of the contents of these books, asserting that since they were found in his house, someone must have sent them to him and that he hadn't opened them.

To further complicate matters, Jordan Chandler provided the police with a description of Jackson's genitals. This led to a deeply humiliating strip search of the star. However, the jury ultimately concluded that the description provided did not match Michael's physical features.

In January, Michael reached a settlement out of court with the Chandlers for $23 million. It's worth noting that no criminal case was ever pursued as there was insufficient evidence aside from Jordan's testimony. In recent times, there have been numerous appalling statements made regarding allegations of inappropriate behavior on my part. I want to emphasize that these statements about me are completely false, as I have consistently maintained from the very beginning. I sincerely hope to be swiftly exonerated from this dreadful ordeal to which I have been subjected.

Michael had become dependent on painkillers, which he took during reconstructive surgeries on his scalp after an injury. He started taking pills again to cope with the stress of the sexual assault allegations that had piled up in the fall of 1993.

He cancelled the remainder of the dangerous tour due to health problems, stress, and dependence on painkillers. By the end of the year, Michael was already tired of a failed relationship and really wanted to start a family. Therefore, the singer proposed to Lisa Marie Presley, daughter of Elvis Presley, by phone. Michael met Lisa when he was 16 and she was six. They grew up and after a private dinner in Los Angeles in 1992, their relationship began. They talked on the phone every day for a year. The couple married on May 26th, 1994, in La Vega, Dominican Republic. It was Michael's first marriage, but unfortunately, it did not last long. The marriage was not just a secret for many weeks, but some facts about their union were quite astonishing. For example, they slept in separate bedrooms despite their on-screen chemistry. The 1994 MTV Video Music Awards are remembered for their marriage. They didn't hesitate to hold hands and kiss in front of 250 million people watching on TV. The worldwide kiss scene led Lisa Marie to believe that Michael used her to make their kiss a topic of conversation for decades.

Lisa Marie did not agree to have children with him because he was emotionally immature. They divorced a year and a half later due to irreconcilable differences, with Lisa Marie thinking that she didn't want to get into a custody battle with him. "I don't want to do this," she was quoted saying. "I don't want to go head-to-head with him, so I need to make sure that everything around is good. I've had certain circumstances; you have to make sure everything's safe and secure, and I wanted to make sure that he and I were really united because we were going to be up against so much!"

In an interview with Oprah, Presley revealed that she and Jackson periodically tried to reconcile in the four years following their divorce, but it was difficult. The tabloids did not stop because of the sex scandal and continued to write that the couple's relationship was not genuine during that time.

Michael was supposed to write the music for the Sega Genesis video game Sonic the Hedgehog 3. However, he left the project when allegations of violence surfaced and went uncredited. He was a fan of Sonic and had previously collaborated with Sega in 1990 on the arcade game Moonwalker. Therefore, for the first time, he felt the unpleasant consequences of the culture of cancellation, which had not yet become a common phenomenon at that time. His musical career was gradually waning, but the performer still had something to contribute to society.

In 1995, Michael released the double album "HIStory: Past, Present and Future, Book I." The first disc, "HIStory Begins," featured top hits and exclusively new compositions. The second disc included a couple of covers. The album became the best-selling multidisc release of all time! However, the song "They Don't Care About Us" from the album drew sharp criticism for using anti-Semitic statements in the lyrics. Specifically, in the original song, the words "Jew me, sue me" caused controversy. Later versions of the song replaced those lyrics with "Do me, sue me."

Shortly after being criticized by the Anti-Defamation League and others, Michael rewrote the lyrics and reissued the song with the changes at the end of the year. While rehearsing for a television performance, Michael suddenly lost consciousness, possibly due to a panic attack caused by stress. He was taken to the hospital. Lisa Marie visited him from time to time, but even then, there was discord between them, ultimately leading to a quick divorce.

Another memorable track on the album was "Earth Song." It gained attention due to an incident that occurred before it topped the UK singles chart on Christmas Eve. Michael was supposed to appear and perform the song at the Brit Awards in 1996. However, his performance was disrupted by pop singer Jarvis Cocker, who protested against Jackson's Christ-like persona. Michael described the scene as disgusting and cowardly. Despite this, the artist embarked on a tour supporting the album, visiting 35 countries and 58 cities, and performing 82 concerts. It became his most attended tour ever.

While visiting Sydney, Australia, the performer married Debbie Rowe at the Sheraton on the Park Hotel. Initially, the couple met when Debbie worked as an assistant to his dermatologist. A friendship developed, and she proposed to Michael that she would be the mother of his children after Lisa Marie Presley refused to have children with him. When Michael divorced Lisa, Debbie

Rowe was six months pregnant with his child, and they subsequently got married.

Michael Joseph Jackson Jr. was born on February 13th, 1997. A year later, the couple had their second child, a girl named Paris Michael Katherine Jackson, born on April 3rd, 1998. Michael Joseph Jackson Jr. later became known as Prince. A team of six nannies and six nurses took care of the boy for the first few months. Debbie, who referred to herself as a private person and rarely gave interviews, was stunned by the publicity and popularity she received after her marriage to Jackson.

Unhappy with the arrangement, Rowe filed for divorce on October 8th, 1999, and initially gave

Michael full custody of the children. However, she would later regain those rights.

Michael released "Blood on the Dance Floor: HIStory in the Mix," which contained only five new songs and was a remix album of singles from HIStory. At that time, Michael Jackson was still a significant figure in the pop music world, but the decline was already being felt. As for the best songs, they are often written effortlessly, as if they somehow write themselves. You don't have to ask for them; they simply drop onto your lap. However, there are also songs that you nurture, planting the seed of an idea and allowing the subconscious to work its magic. Over time, you hope something will come, and most of the time, it does.

Michael worked on his 10th solo album, "Invincible," which cost $30 million to record. From October of that year to September of 2001, he actively participated in charitable movements and projects. In June 1999, Jackson joined Luciano Pavarotti at the War Child charity concert in Modena, Italy. The show raised $1,000,000 for Kosovo war refugees and additional funds for children in Guatemala later that month.

Furthermore, Jackson organized the "Michael Jackson and Friends" benefit concert series in Germany and Korea. The proceeds went to the Nelson Mandela Children's Fund, the Red Cross, and UNESCO. A year later, Guinness World Records honored Michael for helping 39 organizations, more than any other artist, after the September 11th, 2001 attacks.

In response to the attacks, Jackson also helped organize the "United We Stand: What More Can I Give" benefit concert at RFK Stadium in Washington, D.C., which took place on October 21st of that year. In the finale, Jackson performed the track of the same name, "What More Can I Give." The song was specially written by Michael for charity, with contributions from Mariah Carey, Nick Carter, Beyoncé, Céline Dion, Usher, and many more talented artists!

The release of "Invincible" was preceded by a dispute between Michael and his label, Sony Music Entertainment. The singer expected that the licenses for the master recordings of his albums would return to him in the early 2000s, after which he would be able to promote the material as he pleased and keep the profits. However, the clauses of the contract suggested a return date some years later.

Jackson sought early termination of the contract. As a result, "Invincible" was released on October 30th, 2001. It was the first full-length album by Michael Jackson in six years and the last album of original material released by the artist during his lifetime. It debuted at #1 in 13 countries and sold 8 million copies worldwide, going double platinum in the US.

Soon in January, Michael won his 22nd American Music award for Artists of the Century!

Later, an anonymous surrogate mother gave birth to his third child, "Prince" Michael Jackson the 2nd, nicknamed Blanket. In the same year, for some reason, Michael dangled the child by hanging him over the balcony railing in a Berlin hotel room. His room was on the 4th floor. The act drew heavy criticism in the media. Michael apologized, calling the incident a terrible mistake, and explained, "We were waiting for thousands of fans down below, and they were chanting they wanted to see my child, so I was kind enough to let them see. I was doing something out of innocence!"

In April of 2000, one of his last live concerts was performed at the Apollo Theater. It was a benefit concert for the Democratic National Committee and former President Bill Clinton.

However, constant news breaks harmed its reputation in July. Michael called Sony Music chairman Tommy Mottola a racist and accused him of being devilish, someone who exploits black artists for his own gain. Al Sharpton's National Action Network in Harlem launched an investigation into whether Mottola exploited black artists. Jackson also charged that Mottola had referred to his colleague, Irv Gotti, as "that maker". In response, Sony called these statements ridiculous, vicious, and hurtful, and defended Mottola as the man who had supported Michael's career for many years. As a result, Sony refused to renew the contract with the performer.

Michael once said in an interview, "Any painter or sculptor, they paint or sculpt their best work in their 60s or 70s. But in the music business, some of these great artists have become stumped because they abuse themselves and age so prematurely with all these crazy things. They drink and take pills. That's just not good, and it's sad to realize that Michael Jackson was becoming more and more associated with that statement."

Before, the artist's career only slowed down. Now, it collapsed noticeably, and it was almost impossible to avoid it since May of that year when Michael Jackson was filmed for the documentary, "Living with Michael Jackson." British journalist Martin Bashir and his documentary team spent several months with the singer, capturing his life on film.

The film was released on television in February of 2003, and it returned Michael to the violent sex scandal. Bashir persuaded him to discuss his relationship with the children. Jackson said the children continued to sleep at his ranch even after the 1993 allegations. He also said that he sometimes slept with the children in his bed. The film showed Michael holding hands and discussing sleeping conditions with a 12-year-old boy. When questioned, he replied that he didn't see anything wrong with arranging overnight stays with minors and asked, "Why can't you share your bed? That's the most loving thing to do, to share your bed with someone." Michael insisted that the sleepovers were not sexual and that his words were misunderstood. But the media exploded with accusations and controversy.

In December, Santa Barbara authorities charged Jackson with 7 counts of child molestation and two counts of drugging minor Gavin Arvizo with alcoholic beverages. He was also charged with indecent conduct with a minor, attempted indecent conduct with the use of alcohol to facilitate molestation, conspiracy to kidnap a child, false imprisonment, and extortion. Jackson denied the allegations and pleaded not guilty.

The People versus Jackson trial began on January 31st, 2005, in Santa Maria, CA. While the hearing lasted, Michael was highly stressed, which eventually affected his health. The singer lost even more weight by the end of the trial and became a recluse. In May, if convicted, he could face up to 20 years in prison.

As a result, the 2005 trial became a media circus, with fans, detractors, and film crews surrounding the courthouse. More than 130 people testified, including actor Macaulay Culkin, who told the court that he was friends with Jackson as a teenager and never had any problems during his stay at Neverland Ranch.

Jackson's accuser appeared in court on videotape and described how he was given wine and molested. However, the jury noticed inconsistencies in his testimony, as well as in the testimony of his mother. As a result, Michael Jackson was found not guilty of all charges.

Shortly after that, he moved to Bahrain as a personal guest of Sheikh Abdullah. The trial ruined his reputation and his finances fell into despair. Bahrain's prince helped the pop star pay his legal and utility bills and invited him to his country. In Bahrain, the prince took over the singer's expenses and built a recording studio for him. In return, Michael allegedly promised to collaborate with the Al Khalifa label on his new album, write an autobiography, and put on a play. However, the release was never completed, and Jackson soon faced a $7,000,000 lawsuit from his friend for not keeping his promises. He was forced to leave

Bahrain. Moreover, in 2006, Michael faced financial difficulties, and he was urged by financial managers to sell part of his stake in the ATV catalog to avoid bankruptcy.

The main house of Neverland Ranch was closed to save money, and the ranch itself was pledged as collateral for the loan. Approximately 30 Jackson employees did not receive their salaries on time, and wage errors amounted to over $300,000. Jackson was required to pay a $100,000 fine in November of 2006.

Jackson invited the Access Hollywood camera crew into the studio, and MSNBC reported that Michael was working on a new album with a sharp and very talented "Will I Am" producing. On

November 15th, Michael performed "We Are the World" at the World Music Awards in London. He accepted the diamond award for selling over 100 million records, which turned out to be Michael's last public appearance.

In December, he returned to the States and attended the funeral of his biggest inspiration and idol, James Brown. By the fall of 2007, Michael's new album was still in development, and from the new material, Jackson and Sony released "Thriller 25" for the 25th anniversary of the album in 2008. Two remixes were released as singles: "The Girl is Mine" and "Wanna Be Starting Something" 2008. Things got worse as Fortress Investments threatened the artists with foreclosure of the Neverland Ranch, which had been bailed for loans. As a result,

Michael transferred ownership of the Neverland Ranch to the Sycamore Valley Ranch Company LLC and made $35 million. He then arranged for his memorabilia collection of over 1000 items to be sold through Juliano's Auction House.

In March of 2009, amid financial and health rumors, Michael announced a series of "This Is It" comeback concerts at the O2 Arena. The shows would be his first concerts since the 1997 History World Tour. Jackson planned to perform his last concerts and retire after the show. The original plan was to do 10 gigs in London and possibly more gigs in Paris, New York, and Mumbai. The organizer expected to receive about $50 million, but it turned out that Michael's fan base was surprisingly strong.

Michael canceled the auction on the eve of the first public exhibition of the collection of items. He had already made about $200 to $300 million from pre-sales of a series of 10 concerts. they were supposed to take place only in London. Despite all the allegations and stories of bizarre behavior, Jackson remained a figure of great interest. All tickets for the next concerts were sold within the first four hours, but unfortunately, none of them were destined to take place.

After moving to Los Angeles, Jackson rehearsed diligently, trying to perfect the concert program. However, three weeks before the first "This Is It" show on June 25th, 2009, Michael Jackson was using propofol and benzodiazepine.

Conrad Murray, his personal physician, had given Jackson various medications to help him sleep at his rented mansion in Holmby Hills. Boss Angel and Maggie Both changed their clothing, they purchased doctor outfits, and both wore masks and looked like top notch surgeons. Boss Angel rang the bell hoping Doctor Conrad Murray Would not be there. The Boss Angel and Maggie walked into his upstairs bedroom, Michael was barely coherent, He asked both of them I didn't order a doctor or a nurse. At that moment Michael started to convulse. Maggie walked over to Michael's side of the bed and explained to him the situation with the mission and who it was given by. She then told Michael that he has to let us bring you back to good health. Boss Angel then agrees and brings over the IV well

Manny tries to find a vein. Maggie says don't worry Michael will have you dancing and singing in no time, Doctor Conrad will not be returning. Maggie Begins to gain his trust, she tells Michael she's going to give him an injection to guarantee is return to good health. As a few minutes go by, Michael begins to come out of it. but still Maggie tells him to go to the Ronald Reagan UCLA hospital, In the both of us we'll drive you there and stay with you until you come back home, Michael was able to get dressed with the help of Boss Angel who told him to also put a hat and mask on, so he won't be recognized. The more time that went by the stronger Michael became! Boss Angel and Maggie helped Michael get into the van. Michael was becoming a little suspicious and he was wondering where Doctor Conrad was. Boss Angel told Michael, that doctor is not good for you and we are here to save you from him, so let's get you to the hospital and let me worry about Doctor Conrad.

Once Michael was examined the doctor said he's very dehydrated and he needs to put some meat on his bones, other than that he's in pretty good health.

Boss Angel and Maggie bring Michael back to his house, as they pull up Doctor Conrad is sitting in his car, Boss Angel tells Maggie to take Michael's upstairs. Boss Angel walks over to the doctor's car, opens the door and pulls him out by his Collar. Then Boss Angel gets carried away and breaks the jaw of Doctor Conrad. Maggie comes outside and sees Doctor Conrad on the ground holding his Jaw. Maggie looks at Boss Angel and shakes her head come on let's go, our work is done here he's fine, but whenever you work with me again don't you ever pull a stunt like that! Got it?

Boss Angel says I apologize but I just couldn't help it, somebody needed to do that to him, and I don't mind that it was me. Maggie and Boss Angel find themselves back at the Biltmore at the table with the Archangel Achilles. The Boss Angel discuss what had happened in the driveway to the Doctor Conrad.   Achilles said don't worry about it I've got your back on this one. "I Love Billie Jean"

Chapter Eleven

Martin Luther King Jr.

While Boss Angel sits in the lounge at the Biltmore Hotel, waiting for his next mission, Maggie walks in. It's been quite a while since Angel last saw her, and he loves her missions because of the valuable feedback she provides. He's in a great mood until Maggie starts explaining the task. She tells Angel, the boss, that her mission involves the great Martin Luther King Jr.

Boss Angel feels that the murder was unjust and has always felt that way. Maggie realizes that Boss Angel should simply listen to his speech to refresh! It is August 28, 1963 - the March on Washington. *"I have a dream that my four little children will one day live in a nation where they will not be judged by the color of their skin but by the content of their character." "I have a dream that one day this nation will rise up and live out the true meaning of its creed — we hold these truths to be self-evident: that all men are created equal."*

Martin Luther King Jr. begins to travel through the South, hoping to convey his message to the United States government and people of all creeds. During the Montgomery to Selma march, the state police engage in police brutality against the demonstrators. Upon their arrival in Selma, tear gas, billy clubs, and water hoses are used. This police uprising continues from 1963 until 1968.

Maggie's job, assigned by Boss Angel, is to prevent the execution and assassination of Martin Luther King Jr. Maggie tells Boss Angel to go back to April 3rd, 1963, when Martin Luther King Jr. delivered a speech. Boss Angel was present at the speech.

The name of the speech was "I've Been to the Mountaintop!" In King's monologue, there seemed to be a fear of his assassination in his tone. Once he finished and returned to his motel in Tennessee, he would rest for a few days, writing speeches and enjoying time with his children. Boss Angel rents a room four doors down; he knows that today is the day he needs to locate the building where James

Earl Ray will soon attempt to assassinate Martin Luther King.

Boss Angel uses the same method as before to calculate Ray's location and aligns it with a three-story brick building that is a little over two blocks away. As he walks toward the building, he looks up at the top floor and then glances back at the Lorraine Hotel; the angle is perfect.

Meanwhile, Martin Luther and his companions are just arriving back at the hotel. Boss Angel realizes he must hurry. Since the main entrance door is locked, he quickly taps out a glass pane on a window and crawls into the first floor. It turns out to be an auto body shop with no one working. He locates the stairwell and ascends two flights until he reaches the top. The door is slightly ajar, giving the impression that someone had broken in before him.

Too bad Boss Angel is not allowed to carry a firearm; instead, he relies on his experience in stealthy attacks from his days as an ex-mobster. With caution, he slowly pushes the door open and catches a glimpse of James Earl Ray's elbow and shoulder. It appears that Ray is loading a rifle. Suddenly, Ray turns around and notices Boss Angel ducking behind a brick column. Surprisingly, he doesn't shoot but instead rushes towards the window, where he spots Martin Luther King's car without a rear passenger side.

Ray turns his back to Boss Angel, who remains hidden and out of sight. James Earl Ray then points the gun back towards Martin Luther King and his entourage, but he can't quite get the shot he's looking for as they begin ascending the stairs as a group. Ray keeps turning around to keep an eye on Boss Angel, but the opportunity slips away. He turns back around and believes he's finally got the shot, but before he can take it, Boss Angel dives on him. The gun discharges. Then, Ray strikes Boss Angel with the butt of the rifle and flees the building, managing to escape.

Boss Angel feels tempted to take a shot at Ray with his gun, but he realizes he is out of range. Reluctantly, he puts the gun away and wipes it down to remove any fingerprints. He then returns to the hotel where everyone is bewildered by the bullet hole that narrowly missed Martin Luther King but caused no injuries.

Martin Luther King lived to see another day!

I've Been to The Mountaintop

"And then I got into Memphis .and some began to say the threats or talk about the threats that were out what would happen to me from some of our sick white brothers? Well, I don't know what will happen now. We've got some difficult days ahead, but it really doesn't matter with me now because I've been to the mountaintop and I don't mind like anybody, I would like to live a long life. Longevity has its place. But I'm

not concerned about that now. I just want to do God's will. And he's allowed me to go up to the mountain. And I've looked over. And I've seen the promised land. I may not get there with you, but I want you to know tonight that we as the people we'll get to the promised land!"

Boss Angel rises from his seat, clad in an all-white victory suit that he reserves for special occasions. He gives Martin Luther King a heartfelt and enduring standing ovation!

Martin Luther King II finds himself in a hospital battling throat cancer, yet he has served in the state Senate for over a year without much recognition or awareness of his true identity. Despite entering politics relatively recently, it becomes evident to Boss Angel that Martin remains true to his inherent calling. Boss Angel positions himself by Martin's bedside, lost in contemplation.

Chapter Twelve

Marlon Brando

Maggie, what is the mission for today? Marlon Brando's journey into the world of acting commenced at the American Theatre Wing Professional School in New York City. He enrolled and studied there, receiving guidance from the esteemed German director Erwin Piscator, as a member of the Dramatic Workshop at The New School.

During his tenure in New York, Marlon's sisters, Jocelyn and Francis, had already embarked on their respective acting careers. Jocelyn chose to pursue her acting endeavors on Broadway, while Francis focused on studying art in New York. In contrast, Marlon opted for a unique path to channel his creativity.

Marlon Brando gained a reputation for his rebellious nature, often finding himself in troublesome situations. His defiant tendencies became evident when he was expelled from Libertyville High School for riding his motorcycle through the school's corridors. As a consequence, he was enrolled at the Shattuck Military Academy in Minnesota, a school his father had also attended.

Despite his mischievous behavior, Brando demonstrated exceptional talent in both theater and academics. However, his rebellious streak resurfaced in his final year at the academy when he defied a visiting army Colonel during maneuvers, leading to disciplinary actions. Though initially confined to his room, Brando managed to escape and was subsequently apprehended in town. While the faculty advocated for his expulsion, many fellow students sympathized with him and advocated for his reinstatement. In the end, he received an invitation to return the following year, but he ultimately decided to drop out.

After departing from the academy, Marlon Brando took on a summer job as a ditch digger, arranged by his father. Additionally, he made an attempt to enlist in the army, but his application was rejected due to a knee injury he had sustained during his time at Shattuck. Consequently, he was deemed physically unfit for military service and was not accepted into the army.

Finally, Marlon made the decision to follow his sisters' footsteps and pursue acting in New York City. He enrolled in the American Theatre Wing Professional School, where he honed his craft and developed his skills under the guidance of Erwin Piscator. This marks the beginning of Marlon Brando's journey as an actor, which ultimately propelled him to become one of the most renowned and influential actors of the 20th century.

OK, Maggie, why don't you zap us to the set of "The Godfather"? But before that, Boss Angel, I need to brief you on Marlon Brando's career and what has transpired up until this point. It's important to prepare you, as there will be many women constantly around him. While numerous women were infatuated with him, not all of his love affairs evolved into serious relationships. His principles held significant importance to him, to the extent that he even turned down an Oscar. Behind the mask of an eccentric and charismatic rock 'n' roll persona, he carried the weight of grief and wrestling emotions. Today, we will delve into the captivating story of Marlon Brando, a legend in the film industry.

Marlon was raised in Omaha, Nebraska, as the son of Marlon Senior and Dorothy Brando. Marlon inherited his rebellious nature from his mother, who wore pants, smoked, and drove a car in the 1930s. However, Marlon's childhood was somewhat sad. His mother was a heavy drinker and joined Alcoholics Anonymous to address the family issues. Additionally, Marlon experienced sexual abuse by his teenage governess, which resulted in an unhealthy attachment to her.

In 1930, the Brando's moved to Evanston, IL, and Marlon's father found a job in Chicago. Eventually, Marlon's parents separated, and his mother relocated the three children to Santa Ana, California. They later moved to a farm in Libertyville,

IL. Throughout his life, Marlon was consistently told by his friends about his highly expressive facial expressions.

Maggie paused and addressed Boss Angel, "When he made those facial expressions while acting, I'm not certain how it affected other women, but I can tell you what it did for me."

Wow, Maggie! I've never heard you speak about someone in such a manner before. I must say, I'm impressed!

Maggie continued, "Brando was introduced to a neighborhood boy named Wally Cox, who became his lifelong best friend until Cox's death in 2007. In fact, Wally's death deeply affected Marlon. People who knew him at the time believed that he wouldn't be able to recover from it."

After a year, he decided to join the Shattuck Military Academy in Minnesota. He excelled in theatre but continued to display his rebellious nature. However, he dropped out and took a job as a ditch digger. He attempted to enlist in the army, but a football injury prevented him from doing so. Eventually, he found himself in New York to be with his sisters, where he began studying at the American Theatre Wing Professional School. There, he had the opportunity to study under influential German director Erwin Piscator. Marlon enjoyed acting immensely, and in New York, he was accepted and received positive feedback instead of criticism.

Although Brando was couch-surfing, he managed to establish himself as a successful Broadway actor. He achieved further success in the film industry with his roles in the Pulitzer Prize-winning play "A Streetcar Named Desire" and "On The Waterfront." Due to various reasons, he was deemed unfit for military service during the Korean War, thus avoiding it. When questioned about his race by Army officials, he wittily replied, "I am of human color, an oyster white to beige." He also informed the army doctor that he was psychoneurotic and disclosed his expulsion from military school, along with his significant issues regarding authority figures.

Bobby Walason

He met the then-unknown Marilyn Monroe at a party where she played the piano. They would go on to have an intermittent relationship for many years.

Of course, we all remember him for his most famous role in 1972 as Don Vito Corleone in "The Godfather." Maggie, I believe that was the greatest film ever made, one that can never be duplicated.

Well, Boss Angel, you'll appreciate this: Marlon Brando once told a French journalist that homosexuality is so prevalent that it no longer makes news. He expressed that, like many men, he had also experienced homosexuality and he wasn't ashamed of it.

Marlon prepared himself to appear 20 years older than his actual age during the filming of The Godfather. He took responsibility for creating his character. In the presence of Francis Coppola and Paramount executives, right in his living room, he used a shoeshine brush to darken his hair. He used tissue to create jowls on each side of his jaw. He informed the executives that he would speak with a rough voice as he believed the character had been through various experiences. Marlon was truly one of the greatest actors to have ever lived, and he showcased his talent in The Godfather.

When Brando collaborated with Johnny Depp on the film "Don Juan DeMarco," it achieved commercial success despite receiving mixed reviews from critics. Nevertheless, Brando's performance was praised. Additionally, the two actors enjoyed working together and developed a strong friendship. Marlon admired Depp's acting abilities and his grounded demeanor behind the scenes. Likewise, Depp, like many actors, held Brando in high regard. They shared commonalities as they both hailed from working-class families and attained Hollywood success through training and perseverance. They maintained regular phone conversations and even resided in close proximity to each other.

Marlon agreed to star in Depp's directorial debut, the independent neo-western film "The Brave." Depp co-wrote the film with his brother and also acted alongside Brando. The premiere took place at the

Cannes Film Festival in 1997. Unfortunately, the film received unfavorable reviews and was never released in the United States. Brando was also concerned about his inability to highlight the significance of addressing the issue of genocide against indigenous peoples of America.

In his later years, the actor would frequently visit the Neverland Ranch of his close friend, Michael Jackson, where he could relax for weeks. He took part in Michael's 30th-anniversary celebration concert and also featured in his 13-minute video for the song "You Rock My World." Additionally, his son Miko worked as a bodyguard for Jackson for several years, further strengthening their friendship.

In 2004, Marlon Brando signed with Tunisian film director Rita Bahi and began work on a project called "Brando and Brando." However, failing health prevented him from continuing his work.

You see, Boss Angel, Marlon Brando had a serious problem with diabetes that greatly affected his health. Although he was stubborn, his friends and loved ones constantly encouraged him to prioritize his well-being. Maggie suggests that it's time for us to go inside Neverland Ranch.

Boss Angel tells Maggie, "I have the potion from Achilles, but we need to come up with a reason for them to open the gates for us." Maggie suggests, "I've got an idea. Let's say we have a niece and nephew coming to visit who have been here for the past 2 weeks. To make it convincing, we should come up with a name that will guarantee the gates to open. How about Danny Pendergrass? And if they object, Boss Angel, you can create a commotion."

Surprisingly, Maggie utters the name, and the gates open. They proceed to the house on a golf cart with a driver. Once inside, they locate Marlon's whereabouts. Boss Angel prepares the needle and syringe and enters the room, discovering Brando peacefully asleep. However, as Boss Angel approaches Marlon to administer the injection, Michael Jackson walks into the room and inquires, "Who are you? What are you doing here?"

Maggie says, "We are here in search of our cousin, Danny Pendergrass. We dropped him off a week ago and would like to have him back now." Michael Jackson wears a suspicious expression on his face and Maggie adds, "I'll go and fetch Danny."

As soon as Michael exits the room, Boss Angel approaches and injects Brando in his thigh. Maggie urges, "Come on, let's leave now. There's nothing else we can do." After departing the premises, they are left with the hope that the potion will take effect on Brando.

In the following weeks, Brando stars in a new movie alongside Johnny Depp once again. There are reports suggesting that Johnny is telling the media that something remarkable has occurred with Marlon. He's like a completely different person, much younger in spirit with a renewed attitude.

Johnny is ecstatic about whatever transformation has taken place within Marlon Brando.

Chapter Thirteen

Whitney Houston

"It was not a surprise when Whitney Houston began performing in the church choir at the age of 11. During high school, she accompanied her mother at shows and sang backup for other artists. After a brief modeling stint, Houston was discovered by Clive Davis, the founder of Arista Records, in 1983. Although her 1985 debut was not initially successful, several number one singles eventually changed that."

"Maggie, the climb to the top was aided by the Billboard charts. Boss Angel said to Maggie, 'I remember her first pop album, I would listen to it daily and couldn't wait for her next one to be released.' Not to mention how adorable she was, which really helped her pop album reach number one."

The following year, Houston showcased her vocal prowess on the subsequent 'Greatest Love of All' tour, which truly launched a long run supported by the majority of her albums and similar tours.

Thereafter, in 1987, the massively successful Whitney Houston became the first female artist to have an album premiere at the top of the Billboard Chart. It spawned several number one hits, including a Grammy-winning single that catapulted her into global stardom. In 1990, she also achieved an Emmy-winning track for the 1988 Summer Olympics and established a children's charity. Despite the album's urban feel and combination of ballads and energetic tracks, it didn't sell as well as her previous work. However, Houston still achieved a top 20 hit with her recording of the American National Anthem for Super Bowl 25. It was rumored to hold the record as the number one anthem, even surpassing Marvin Gaye's incredible rendition.

When the charity single was released in the wake of 9/11, it reached a spot within the top 10. Houston was busy in 1992 following her marriage to singer Bobby Brown of New Edition fame.

She made her film debut in the romantic thriller 'The Bodyguard.' Maggie, watching 'The Bodyguard' made me fall in love with her. Partly because of Kevin Costner, but mainly because her acting skills truly showcased the talent Whitney possessed. I actually watched that movie, Maggie, four to five times. Boss Angel, you were not alone. It had culture, and it even reminded me somewhat of you! 'The Bodyguard' did so well that it brought recognition to Whitney as a triple threat. The box office hit was not only huge but also a Grammy-winning album that became the best-selling soundtrack in history. It included the chart-topping cover of Dolly Parton's song, which eventually became Houston's signature tune. After 'The

Bodyguard,' Whitney certainly grew in stature. Maggie says to Boss Angel, "There were plenty of rumors during the second half of filming that she and Kevin Costner had a thing going on." However, there was never any solid evidence, and both of them chose to remain silent about it, if it indeed did happen!

Next on Houston's list, she joined the all African American cast of the number one movie, "Waiting to Exhale." The film's hit soundtrack featured Houston's Grammy-winning and chart-topping single, "Exhale (Shoop Shoop)," along with contributions from other African American artists. In 1996, she continued her success in the film and soundtrack of "The Preacher's Wife," which made

Houston the highest-paid African American actress in Hollywood at the time, earning a $10 million payday. The corresponding soundtrack became one of the best-selling gospel records in history. Boss Angel, Maggie, can you believe how far she had climbed to earn $10 million for one film? And just imagine the wealth amassed throughout her singing career!

Boss Angel, hey, did you see Whitney in the 1997 play "The Fairy Godmother"? It was a TV remake of the musical Cinderella by a production company. She also paid homage to some of her influences in a concert series titled "Classic Whitney Houston."

No, Maggie, I didn't see it, but I heard about it. That was during my heyday in Providence.

Whitney returned to non-movie-related work with her 1998 album, "My Love Is Your Love," which was commercially and critically acclaimed as a masterpiece. Her collaborative effort with Mariah Carey, featured on the "Prince of Egypt" soundtrack, earned them both an Oscar nomination. The following year, Houston performed on VH1's "Divas Live."

However, her personal life was suffering. Marriage troubles, substance abuse issues, and unreliable behavior tainted her reputation. She addressed these issues in an interview with Diane Sawyer. After signing a $100 million deal with Arista BMG, Houston released the album "Just Whitney" which reached the top ten, and the Christmas record "One Wish: The Holiday Album."

She also appeared on her husband's reality show, "Being Bobby Brown," which exposed many of the couple's problems and eventually led to their divorce in 2007.

Whitney Houston's final album was 2009's Billboard-topping "I Look to You." Unfortunately, Houston's concerts on the Nothing but Love World Tour received negative feedback, and certain dates were called off following a period in rehab. Her best friend, Robin, who some say was also her love, was the glue that held it together. Boss Angel tells Maggie that he believes if the divorce had happened years earlier, and Robin was able to guide Whitney, her career would have only strengthened instead of weakened. "You're right, Boss Angel. I agree with you. But now it's up to us to bring her back, despite herself and her situation!"

Whitney starred in the movie "Sparkle." However, there was a premiere where Boss Angel and Maggie had to intervene in the outcome. Houston was staying in a suite at the Beverly Hilton Hotel in California, which was also the venue for the event. Maggie and Boss Angel had to come up with a plan to save her from the potential danger that awaited her. The Boss had an idea - he instructed Maggie to go to the basement, find the maids' quarters, put on a maid's outfit, and meet him on the 9th floor at Room 908 where they would wait for him.

Meanwhile, Boss Angel had to ensure that the security team had no knowledge of their plan. So, he took the elevator to the 9th floor where he encountered Maggie dressed in a cute maid's outfit, complete with a name tag that read "Marilyn." Boss Angel tried knocking on the door, but there was no response. He noticed a maid walking down the hallway and instructed Maggie to approach her. Boss Angel advised Maggie to explain that she had lost her key to Room 908 and it wasn't working. She should then ask if the maid had a master key to grant them access. However, the maid responded, "I can't provide you with access to that room! You'll need to go to the front desk for assistance!"

At that moment, Boss Angel said, "I'm the security for this client," and pulled out his badge, which startled the maid. She then retrieved her master key and unlocked the deadbolt. Boss Angel thanked her and said, "We'll take it from here." Maggie and Boss Angel entered the room to find Whitney face down naked in the tub. Boss Angel swiftly picked her up in his arms and carried her to the bed, turning her onto her back. He began performing CPR, giving mouth-to-mouth, but there was no response. He turned to Maggie and asked for the potion from Achilles. Maggie hesitated, explaining that giving someone a double dose had never been done before. Boss Angel insisted, "I don't care. Give me another dose, or we're going to lose her anyway!" Maggie reluctantly refilled the syringe. Boss Angel inserted it directly into Whitney's heart. Suddenly, Whitney began taking strong breaths, and her eyes opened. Confused, she looked at both of them and asked, "Who are you?

Why are you here? I'm supposed to be paying tribute to myself at the 54th Grammy Awards and promoting my movie 'Sparkle'."

Boss Angel, together with Maggie, saved her from certain death! Whitney Houston continued on with her incomparable voice and the versatility that allowed her to tackle multiple musical styles and genres with incredible strength. Whitney Houston became one of the most popular female artists in history. Her success paved the way for future black female stars, and her music has since influenced singers from all backgrounds. Whitney refrained from using drugs and alcohol, and the public couldn't figure out what her secret was. Little did they know, she got by with a little help from the Boss Angel, and not to mention my angel Maggie!

ABOUT ROBERT WALASON PUBLISHING

This is the third edition of the Boss Angel series. Also available from Author; Bobby Walason, Boss Angel, Boss Angel II, UnMade Honor Loyalty Redemption and soon to be released, Boss Angel Comic Book series.

Contact us:

unmade2@gmail.com

unmade.org

ROBERT WALASON PUBLISHING